SWU-700-005

UNIFORMS OF RUSSIAN ARMY IN THE XVIII CENT. VOL.1

UNDER THE REIGN OF CATHERINE II EMPRESSE OF RUSSIA BETWEEN 1762 AND 1796

From the Viskovatov's greatest work:
"Historical description of the clothing and
arms of the Russian Army"

SOLDIERSHOP PUBLISHING

AUTHOR

Aleksandr Vasilevich Viskovatov born 22 April (4 May New Style) 1804, died 27 February (11 March) 1858 in St. Petersburg, Russian military historian. He graduated from the 1st Cadet Corps and served in the artillery, the hydrographic depot of the Naval Ministry, and then in the Department of Military Educational Institutions. He mainly studied historical artifacts and the histories of military units. Viskovatov's greatest work was the Historical Description of the Clothing and Arms of the Russian Army.

Title: **UNIFORMS OF RUSSIAN ARMY IN THE XVIII Cent. VOL. 1 -**
The Russian Army under the reign of Catherine the Great 1762-1796
By A.V. Viskovatov. Serie edit by Luca S. Cristini. First edition by Soldiershop. September 2016
Cover & Art Design: Luca S. Cristini. Plates re-colorations by Anna Cristini.
ISBN code: 978-88-93271189
Published by Soldiershop publishing, via Padre Davide, 7 - 24050 Zanica (BG) ITALY. www.soldiershop.com

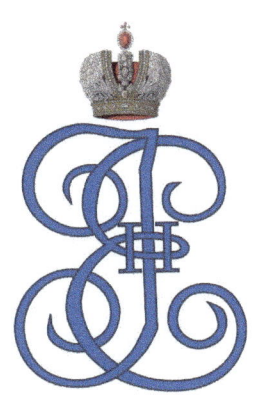

UNIFORMS
OF THE RUSSIAN ARMY IN
THE XVIII Cent.
VOL.1

UNDER THE REIGN OF CATHERINE II EMPRESSE OF
RUSSIA BETWEEN 1762 AND 1796

Catherine II of Russia also known as Catherine the Great 21 April 1729 – 6 November 1796)

HISTORICAL DESCRIPTION OF THE CLOTHING AND ARMS
OF THE RUSSIAN ARMY - A.V. VISKOVATOV

Soldiershop is glad to presents the complete collection of the great job made by A.V. Viskovatov dedicated to the uniforms and weapons belonging from the first Zar and Russian emperors to the Russian army during the Napoleonic period, until 1860 about. The time we considered in this volume corresponds to the reigns of Catherine the Great (Catherine II) who reigned since 1762 until his murder on the 6 November 1796.

Our reprint in based on the original 19th century volumes, to be precise the volumes from 4 to 6 are dedicated to the reign of Catherine II; this part is distributed on 3 or 4 volumes.

Our new edition, the first ever published in English, both on paper and digital format, boasts a large number of color plates, many of them unpublished and re-coloured by our team of expert artists and scholars of uniformology. Each volume is based on 100 color plates or more, always accompanied by the original translated text which describes the subjets of the plates.

A unique work in its genre, a must have in any respecting collection!

Aleksandr Vasilevich Viskovatov born 22 April (4 May New Style) 1804, died 27 February (11 March) 1858 in St. Petersburg, Russian military historian. He graduated from the 1st Cadet Corps and served in the artillery, the hydrographic depot of the Naval Ministry, and then in the Department of Military Educational Institutions.

He mainly studied historical artifacts and the histories of military units. Viskovatov's greatest work was the Historical Description of the Clothing and Arms of the Russian Army (Vols. 1-30, St. Petersburg, 1841-62; 2nd ed. Vols. 1-34, St. Petersburg - Novosibirsk - Leningrad, 1899-1948). This work is based on a great quantity of archival documents and contains four thousand colored illustrations.

Viskovatov was the author of Chronicles of the Russian Army (Books 1-20, St. Petersburg, 1834-42) and Chronicles of the Russian Imperial Army (Parts 1-7, St. Petersburg, 1852). He collected valuable material on the history of the Russian navy which went into A Short Overview of Russian Naval Campaigns and General Voyages to the End of the XVII Century (St. Petersburg, 1864; 2nd edition Moscow, 1946). Together with A.I. Mikhailovskii-Danilevskii he helped prepare and create the Military Gallery in the Winter Palace.

He wrote the historical military inscriptions for the walls of the Hall of St. George in the Great Palace of the Kremlin. (From the article in the Soviet Military Encyclopedia.)

CONTENTS

MEMOIRS OF THE EMPRESS CATHERINE II
WRITTEN BY HERSELF - PART I.

FROM 1729, THE YEAR OF HER BIRTH, TO 1751

Fortune is not so blind as people think. Her movements are often the result of precise and well-planned measures, which escape the perception of common minds; still oftener are they the result of personal qualities, character, and conduct. To render this more evident, I will propose the following syllogism:
Qualities and character shall form the major Conduct, the minor; Good or evil fortune, the conclusion.
Here are two striking illustrations:
PETER III
CATHERINE II
PETER III, HIS FATHER AND MOTHER.

The mother of Peter III was a daughter of Peter I. Two months after the birth of her son she died of consumption, in the little town of Kiel, in Holstein, a victim to grief at finding herself established in such a place and married so badly. Charles Frederic, Duke of Holstein, nephew of Charles XII, King of Sweden, was the father of Peter III. He was a weak prince, ugly, little, sickly, and poor (see the Journal of Berkholz, in Busching's Magazine). He died in 1739, leaving his son, not quite eleven years old, under the guardianship of his cousin, Adolphus Frederic, Bishop of Lubeck and Duke of Holstein, since elected King of Sweden, in consequence of the peace of Abo, and the recommendation of the Empress Elizabeth. The education of Peter III was placed under the superintendence of the Grand Marshal of his Court, Brummer, a Swede by birth, under whom were the Great Chamberlain Berkholz, author of the journal just alluded to, and four chamberlains, two of whom, Adlerfeldt, author of a history of Charles XII, and Wachmeister, were Swedes, and the other two, Wolff and Madfeldt, natives of Holstein. The Prince was educated for the throne of Sweden, in a court too large for the country which contained it; and this court was divided into several factions mutually hating each other, each seeking to obtain an ascendancy over the mind of the Prince, instead of endeavouring to form his character, and all bent upon inspiring him with an aversion for those opposed to them. The young Prince cordially hated Brummer; nor did he like any of his attendants, because they kept him under restraint.

Even from the ago of ten, Peter III showed a fondness for drink. He had to submit to numerous presentations, and was never out of sight night or day. The persons he most liked during his childhood and the first years of his residence in Russia were two old valets de chambre—Cramer, a Livonian, and Roumberg, a Swede. The latter was the favourite; he was a somewhat rough and vulgar person, who had been a dragoon under Charles XII. Brummer, and consequently Berkholz, who only saw with the eyes of Brummer, was attached to the Prince Guardian and Administrator; all the rest were dissatisfied with this Prince, and still more so with his adherents.

When the Empress Elizabeth ascended the throne of Russia, she sent the Chamberlain Korf into Holstein to demand her nephew. In consequence, the Prince Administrator immediately sent him off, accompanied by the Grand Marshal Brummer, the Chamberlain Berkholz, and the Chamberlain Decken, nephew of the former. The Empress received the Prince with great joy, and soon after his arrival set out for Moscow to be crowned. She had determined to declare him her heir; but, first of all, it was indispensable that he should be received into the Greek church. The enemies of the Grand Marshal Brummer, and particularly the Great Chamberlain Count Bestoujeff and the Count M. Panin, who was for a long time Russian minister in Sweden, pretended to have in their possession convincing proofs that Brummer, from the moment he found the Empress determined to declare her nephew heir presumptive to her throne, took as much pains to corrupt the mind and heart of his pupil as he had before taken to render him worthy of the crown of Sweden. But I have always doubted this atrocity, and looked upon the education of Peter III as a conflict of unfortunate circumstances. I will relate what I have seen and heard, and even that will explain a great deal.

I saw Peter III for the first time when he was eleven years old. He was then at Eutin with his guardian, the Prince Bishop of Lubeck, some months after the death of his father, the Duke Charles Frederic. The Prince Bishop had assembled all his family at Eutin, in 1739, in order to meet his ward. My grandmother, mother of the Prince Bishop, and my mother, his sister, had come from Hamburg with me. I was then ten years old. Prince Augustus and the Princess Anne, brother and sister of the Prince Guardian and Administrator of Holstein, were also there; and it was then I heard it stated, in the presence of the assembled family, that the young Duke was inclined to drink, his attendants finding it difficult to prevent him from getting intoxicated at table; that he was restive and impetuous; without affection for those about him, and especially disliking Brummer; that, otherwise, he was not wanting in vivacity, but that he was of a weak and sickly constitution. In point of fact, his complexion was pale, and he appeared thin and delicate. To this child his attendants wished to give the appearance of a complete man; and for this purpose he was tormented with restraints only calculated to teach him falsehood as well in character as in deportment.

The little court of Holstein had not long been settled in Russia when an embassy arrived from Sweden, requesting the Empress to allow her nephew to be placed on the throne of that kingdom. Elizabeth, however, had already announced her intentions by the preliminaries of the peace of Abo, as previously mentioned; and she replied to the Swedish diet that she had declared her nephew heir to the throne of Russia, and that she adhered to the preliminaries of the peace of Abo, which gave to Sweden, as heir presumptive to the crown, the Prince Administrator of Holstein. (This Prince had had an elder brother, to whom the Empress had been affianced at the death of Peter I. The marriage had not taken place, as the Prince died of small-pox a few weeks after the betrothal; but the Empress retained much affection for his memory, as she showed by many marks of favour to all the family.)

Peter III, then, was declared heir to Elizabeth and Grand Duke of Russia, after having previously made his profession of faith according to the rites of the Greek church. His instructor on this occasion was Simon Theodorsky, since Archbishop of Pleskov. The Prince had been baptized and brought up in the Lutheran creed in its most rigid and least tolerant form. He had always been refractory under instruction of every kind; and I have heard his attendants say that, while at Kiel, they had infinite trouble in getting him to church on Sundays and holidays, and making him perform the acts of devotion required of him; and that most of the time he displayed his irreligion in the presence of Simon Theodorsky. His Royal Highness took it into his head to dispute upon every point, and his attendants had often to be called in to check his ill-humour or impetuosity. At last, after giving a deal of trouble, he submitted to the wishes of his aunt the Empress; though, whether from prejudice, habit, or the spirit of contradiction, he frequently took care to let it be seen that he would rather have gone to Sweden than remain in Russia. He retained Brummer, Berkholz, and his Holstein attendants until his marriage. Some other masters were added to these as a matter of routine: Mr. Isaac Wesselowsky for the Russian language; he came but rarely at first, and finally not at all; the other was the Professor Stehlein, who was to teach him mathematics and history, but who, in reality, only played with him, and served him as a buffoon. The person who was most assiduous was the ballet-master, Laudé, who taught him dancing.

1744

At first, the sole occupation of the Grand Duke, when in his private apartment, was to make the two servants who attended him there to go through the military exercise. He gave them titles and ranks, and then again degraded them, according to the whim of the moment. It was truly child's play, and a constant childhood. In general, indeed, he was very childish, although at this time he was sixteen. In 1744, while the court was at Moscow, Catherine II arrived there with her mother, on the 9th of February.

The Russian court was at that time divided into two great sections or parties. At the head of the first, which now began to recover from its previous depression, was the Vice-Chancellor Count Bestoujeff Rumine. He was a man far more feared than loved, excessively intriguing and suspicious, firm and resolute in his principles, not a little tyrannical, an implacable enemy, but a steady friend, never abandoning those who did not first turn their backs on him. He was, besides, difficult to get along with, and apt to stand upon trifles. He was at the head of the department of foreign affairs. Having to contend with those immediately about the Empress, he had been kept down before the journey to Moscow; but now he began to gain an ascendancy. He leaned to the court of Vienna, to that of Saxony, and to England. The arrival of Catherine II and her mother gave him no pleasure; it was the secret work of the faction opposed to him. The enemies of the Count were numerous, but he made them all tremble. He had over them the advantage of his position and character, which gave him great weight in the politics of the ante-chamber.

The party opposed to Bestoujeff were in favour of France, her protégée Sweden, and the king of Prussia. The Marquis de la Chétardie was the soul of this party; the courtiers from Holstein its prominent personages. They had gained over Lestocq, one of the principal actors in the revolution which had placed Elizabeth on the throne of Russia. He had a large share in her confidence. He had been her surgeon since the death of the Empress Catherine I, to whose household he had also been attached, and had rendered essential services to both mother and daughter. He was not wanting either in shrewdness, skill, or intrigue; but he was malicious, and had a bad heart. All these strangers supported him, and put forward Count Michael Woronzoff, who had also taken part in the revolution, and had accompanied Elizabeth on the night she ascended the throne. She had made him marry the niece of the Empress Catherine I, the Countess Anna Karlovna Skavronsky, who had been brought up with herself, and was very much attached to her. To this faction also belonged the Count Alexander Roumianzoff, father of the Marshal, who had signed the peace of Abo with Sweden—a peace in which Bestoujeff had been but little consulted. The party also counted upon the Procurator-general Troubetzkoy, upon the whole Troubetzkoy family, and, consequently, upon the Prince of Hesse-Homburg, who had married a princess of this family. The Prince of Hesse-Homburg, who was much thought of at that time, was personally of little consequence, his importance being wholly derived from the extensive family to which his wife belonged, and of which the father and mother were still living: the latter enjoyed great consideration.

The remaining portion of those who were about the Empress consisted at that time of the family of Schouvaloff. These balanced in all respects the Master of the Hounds, Razoumowsky, who, for the moment, was the acknowledged favourite.

Count Bestoujeff knew how to make these latter useful, but his chief reliance was on the Baron Tcherkassoff, Secretary of the Cabinet to the Empress, and who had previously served in the cabinet of Peter I. He was a rough and headstrong man, an advocate of order and justice, and one who wished to see everything in due form and system. The remainder of the court took sides with one or other of these parties, according to their several interests or personal feelings.

The arrival of my mother and myself seemed to give the Grand Duke much pleasure. I was then in my fifteenth year. During the first few days he showed me great attention. Even then, and in that short time, I could see that he cared but little for the nation over which he was destined to rule; that he leaned to Lutheranism; that he had no affection for those about him; and that he was very childish. I was silent, and listened, and this gained me his confidence. I remember his telling me, among other things, that what most pleased him in me was, that I was his cousin, as he could therefore, from our near relationship, open his heart to me with entire confidence; and hereupon he went on to inform me that he was in love with one of the maids of honour to the Empress, who had been dismissed from court in consequence of the misfortune of her mother, a Madame Lapoukine, who had been exiled to Siberia; that he would have been very glad to have married her, but that he was resigned to marry me instead, as his aunt wished it. I listened with a blush to these family disclosures, thanking him for his premature confidence; but, in reality, I was astounded at his imprudence and utter want of judgment in a variety of matters.

The tenth day after my arrival in Moscow, it was Saturday, the Empress went to the convent of Troïtza. The Grand Duke remained with us at Moscow. Three masters had already been assigned me: Simon Theodorsky, to instruct me in the Greek faith; Basil Adadouroff, for the Russian language; and the ballet-master, Laudé, for dancing. In order to make greater progress in the Russian, I used to sit up in bed when every one else was asleep, and learned by heart the lessons which Adadouroff had left me. As my room was warm, and I had no experience of the climate, I neglected to put on my shoes or stockings, but studied just as I left my bed. The consequence was, that from the fifteenth day I was seized with a pleurisy which threatened to kill me. It commenced with a shivering, which seized me on the Tuesday after the departure of the Empress for the convent of Troïtza, just as I had dressed for dinner. My mother and myself were to dine that day with the Grand Duke, and I had much difficulty in getting her to allow me to go to bed. On her return from dinner, she found me almost without consciousness, in a burning fever, and with an excruciating pain in the side. She fancied I was going to have the small-pox; sent for the physicians, and wished me to be treated in consequence. The medical men insisted on my being bled, but she would not listen to the proposal, saying that it was from being bled that her brother had died of the small-pox in Russia, and that she did not wish me to share the same fate. The physicians, and the attendants of the Grand Duke, who had not had the disease, sent to the Empress an exact report of the state of matters, and in the mean time, while my mother and the doctors were disputing, I lay in my bed, unconscious, in a burning fever, and with a pain in the side which occasioned intense suffering, and forced from me continual moanings, for which my mother scolded me, telling me that I ought to bear my sufferings patiently.

Finally, on the Saturday evening, at seven o'clock, that is, on the fifth day of my disease, the Empress returned from the convent at Troïtza, and, on alighting from her carriage, proceeded to my room, and found me without consciousness. She had with her Count Lestocq and a surgeon, and having heard the opinion of the physicians, she sat down at the head of my bed, and ordered me to be bled. The moment the blood came, I recovered my consciousness, and, opening my eyes, found myself in the arms of the Empress, who had lifted me up. For twenty-seven days I lay between life and death, and during that period I was bled sixteen times, on some occasions as often as four times in the day. My mother was scarcely ever allowed to enter my room. She continued opposed to these frequent bleedings, and loudly asserted that the doctors were killing me. She began, however, to believe that I should not have the small-pox. The Empress had placed the Countess Roumianzoff and several other ladies in attendance on me, and it seemed that my mother's judgment was distrusted. At last, under the care of the physician Sanches, a Portuguese, the abscess which had formed in my right side burst. I vomited it, and from that moment I began to recover. I soon perceived that my mother's conduct during my illness had lowered her in every one's estimation. When she saw me very bad, she wished a Lutheran clergyman to be brought to me. I have been told that they brought me to myself, or took advantage of a moment of returning consciousness, to propose this to me, and that I replied, "What is the good? I would rather have Simon Theodorsky; I will speak to him with pleasure." He was brought, and addressed me in a manner that gave general satisfaction. This occurrence did me great service in the opinion of the Empress and of the entire court. There was also another circumstance which injured my mother. One day, towards Easter, she took it into her head to send me word by a maid-servant that she wished me to give up to her a piece of blue and silver stuff, which my father's brother had presented to me on my departure for Russia, seeing that I had taken a great fancy for it. I replied that she could, of course, take it, though I certainly prized it very much, as my uncle had given it to me because I liked it so much. The persons about me perceiving that I parted with it unwillingly, and considering how long I had hovered between life and death, having only got a little better within the last two or three days, began to complain of my mother's imprudence in giving any annoyance to a dying child, saying, that so far from depriving me of my dress, she ought not even to have mentioned the matter. The circumstance was related to the Empress, who instantly sent me several superb pieces of stuff, and among them one of blue and silver, but the circumstance injured my mother in the estimation of the Empress. She was accused of having no affection for me, nor any discretion either. I had accustomed myself during my illness to lie with my eyes closed. I was supposed to be asleep, and then the Countess Roumianzoff, and the ladies who were with her, spoke their minds freely, and I thus learned a great many things.

As I began to get better, the Grand Duke often came to spend the evening in my mother's apartment, which was also mine. He and every one else seemed to take the greatest interest in my condition. The Empress had often shed tears about me. At last, on the 21st of April, 1744, my birthday, whence commenced my fifteenth year, I was able to appear in public for the first time after this severe illness.

I fancy that people were not much edified with the apparition. I was wasted away to a skeleton. I had grown; but my face and features had lengthened, my hair had fallen off, and I was deadly pale. To myself I looked frightfully ugly; I could not recognize myself. The Empress sent me, on the occasion, a pot of rouge, and ordered me to use it.

With the return of spring and fine weather, the assiduities of the Grand Duke ceased. He preferred walking and shooting in the environs of Moscow. Sometimes, however, he came to dine or sup with us, and then he continued his childish confidences to me, while his attendants conversed with my mother, who received much company, and with whom many conferences took place, which did not fail to displease those who were not present at them, especially Count Bestoujeff, all whose enemies were in the habit of assembling with us, and particularly the Marquis de la Chétardie, who had not yet put forth any character from the court of France, though he carried in his pocket his credentials as ambassador.

In the month of May, the Empress again visited the convent of Troïtza, whither the Grand Duke, myself, and my mother followed her. For some time the Empress had begun to treat my mother with much coldness. At the convent of Troïtza, the reason for this became apparent. One afternoon, when the Grand Duke was in our room, the Empress entered suddenly, and desired my mother to follow her into the other apartment. Count Lestocq followed there also.

The Grand Duke and I sat upon a window-sill, waiting. The conversation lasted a long time. At last, Count Lestocq came out, and, in passing, came near the place where the Grand Duke and I were sitting laughing, and said to us, "This merriment will soon cease." And then, turning to me, he added, "You may pack up: you are going to set off home at once." The Grand Duke wished to know the reason of this. "You will learn afterwards," was the reply of the Count, who departed to fulfil the commission with which he was charged, and of the nature of which I was ignorant. The Grand Duke and myself were left to ruminate on what we had heard. His commentaries were in words; mine in thoughts. "But," he said, "if your mother is in fault, you are not." I answered, "My duty is to follow my mother, and do what she orders me." I saw plainly that he would have parted from me without regret. As for myself, considering his character and sentiments, the matter was nearly indifferent to me also, but the crown of Russia was not so. At last the door of the bed-room opened, and the Empress came out with a flushed face and an angry look. My mother followed her, her eyes red, and filled with tears. As we scrambled down from the window where we were perched, and which was rather high, the Empress smiled. She then kissed us both, and departed. When she had gone, we learned pretty nearly how matters stood.

The Marquis de la Chétardie, who formerly, or, to speak more correctly, in his first diplomatic journey to Russia, had stood very high in the favour and confidence of the Empress, found himself, in his second journey, fallen from his hopes. His conversations were more measured than his letters; these were filled with the most rancorous bitterness. They had been opened, deciphered. In them were found the details of his conversations with my mother, and with many other persons, relative to the affairs of the empire, and to the Empress herself; and as the Marquis had not displayed any character, the order was given for expelling him from the empire. The badge of the order of St. Andrew and the portrait of the Empress were taken from him; but he was allowed to retain all the other presents of jewels made him by her Majesty. I do not know whether my mother succeeded in justifying herself in the mind of the Empress, but at all events, we did not go away. However, my mother continued to be treated with much reserve and coldness. I do not know what passed between her and La Chétardie, but I know that one day he complimented me on my having my hair arranged *en Moyse*. I replied that to satisfy the Empress, I would dress my hair in every style that could give her pleasure. When he heard this he turned on his heel, went off in another direction, and did not again speak to me.

On our return from Moscow with the Grand Duke, my mother and I were more isolated. Fewer people came to see us, and I was being prepared for making my profession of faith. The 28th of June was fixed for this ceremony, and the following day, the Feast of St. Peter, for my betrothal with the Grand Duke. I remember that Marshal Brummer, several times during this period, complained to me of his pupil, and wished to make use of me for correcting or reproving him; but I told him it was impossible for me to do so, and that were I to attempt it I should only render myself as odious to him as his attendants were already.

During this period, my mother became very intimate with the Prince and Princess of Hesse, and still more so with the brother of the latter, the Chamberlain Retsky. This connection displeased the Countess Roumianzoff, Marshal Brummer, and, in fact, every one; and, while she was engaged with them in her room, the Grand Duke and I were making a racket in the ante-chamber, of which we were in full possession; we were neither of us wanting in youthful vivacity.

In the month of July, the Empress celebrated, at Moscow, the peace with Sweden. On this occasion, a Court was formed for me, as an affianced Grand Duchess of Russia; and, immediately after the celebration, the Empress sent us off for Kiev. She set out herself some days later. We made short stages—my mother and I, the Countess Roumianzoff, and one of the ladies of my mother's suite in one carriage; the Grand Duke, Brummer, Berkholz, and Decken in another. One afternoon, the Grand Duke, tired of being with his pedagogues, wished to join my mother and me. Once in with us, he would not leave our carriage. Then my mother, wearied with being always with him and me, took a fancy to augment our company. She communicated her idea to the young people of our suite, among whom were Prince Galitzine, since Marshal of this name, and Count Zachar Czernicheff. One of the carriages, containing our beds, was taken, benches were ranged all round it, and the next morning the Grand Duke, my mother and I, Prince Galitzine, Count Czernicheff, and one or two more of the youngest of the suite, entered it. And thus we passed the rest of our journey very gaily, as far as our carriage life was concerned; but all who were not with us protested against the arrangement. It extremely displeased the Grand Marshal Brummer, the Great Chamberlain Berkholz, the Countess Roumianzoff, the Lady-in-waiting on my mother, and, in fact, all the rest of the suite, because they were never admitted; and, while we laughed through the journey, they were grumbling and wearied.

In this manner we reached Koselsk, at the end of three weeks, and there remained three other weeks waiting for the Empress, who had been delayed on her route by several occurrences. We learnt at Koselsk that during her journey several persons of her suite had been sent into exile, and that she was in very bad humour. At last, about the middle of August, she reached Koselsk, and we remained there with her till the end of the month. While there, the people played at faro from morning till night, in a large hall in the centre of the house, and they played high. We were all much cramped in point of space. My mother and I slept in the same room, the Countess Roumianzoff and the Lady-in-waiting on my mother in the ante-chamber, and so on with the others. One day, when the Grand Duke came into our room, my mother was writing, while her casket lay open at her side. The Duke, from curiosity, wanted to rummage in the casket; my mother told him not to touch it; and, in point of fact, he moved away and went capering about the place. But while leaping here and there in order to make me laugh, he caught the lid of the casket and upset it. Then my mother got angry, and hard words passed between them. She accused him of having upset the casket on purpose; he denied this, and complained of her injustice. Both appealed to me. Knowing my mother's temper, I was afraid of getting my ears boxed if I did not side with her; and, on the other hand, I did not wish to tell a falsehood or displease the Grand Duke, so that I was between two fires. However, I told my mother that I did not think the Duke had done it intentionally, but that, while leaping, his dress had caught the lid of the casket, which stood on a very small stool. Then my mother took me in hand, for when she was angry she must have some one to find fault with. I was silent and began to cry. The Grand Duke finding that all my mother's anger fell upon me, because I had testified in his favour, and seeing me in tears, accused her of injustice and of being mad with passion; to which she retorted by calling him a very ill-behaved little boy. In a word, it would have been difficult to go farther than they did without actually coming to blows. From this moment the Grand Duke took a dislike to my mother; nor did he ever forget this quarrel. She, on the other hand, retained a grudge against him, and their behaviour to each other tended to produce restraint, distrust, and bitterness. They seldom concealed their feelings when with me, and it was in vain that I sought to soften them towards each other. I never succeeded beyond the moment, and that but rarely. They had always some sarcasm ready for annoyance, and my situation became every day more painful. I tried to obey the one and please the other; and, indeed, at that time the Grand Duke gave me his confidence more completely than he did to any one else; for he saw that my mother often took me to task, when she was unable to fasten upon him. This, of course, did me no harm in his estimation, for he felt that he could count upon me.

Finally, on the 29th of August we reached Kiev. We remained there ten days, and then set out for Moscow, travelling in precisely the same manner as before.

Having arrived at Moscow, the entire autumn was passed in dramatic representations, ballets, and court masquerades. In spite of all this, however, it was evident that the Empress was often in bad humour. One day while at the theatre, my mother, the Grand Duke, and I, being in a box opposite her Majesty, I perceived the Empress speaking very warmly and angrily to Count Lestocq. When she had ended, the Count left her and came to our box. Approaching me he said, "Have you seen how the Empress spoke to me?" I answered that I had. "Very well, then," he said; "she is very angry with you." "With me! and why?" I replied. "Because," he said, "you are much in debt. She says that wells may be dried up; that when she was a princess she had no greater allowance than you have, though she had an establishment to provide for; and that she took care not to get into debt, because she knew that no one would pay for her." All this he uttered in a dry tone and with an air of displeasure, apparently that the Empress might see from her box how he had executed his commission. Tears came into my eyes, and I was silent. Having finished what he had to say, the Count departed. The Grand Duke, who was seated at my side, heard most of the conversation; and after questioning me relative to the remainder, he gave me to understand, rather by looks than words, that he agreed with his aunt and was not sorry I had been scolded. This was his general way of acting, and he fancied he should thus render himself agreeable to the Empress by entering into her views when she was angry with any one. My mother also, when she learnt what had happened, said it was only the natural consequence of the pains that had been taken to withdraw me from her control; and that since they had put me in a condition to act without consulting her, she should wash her hands of the matter. Thus they both took part against me.

As for me, I determined instantly to put my affairs into order; and the next morning I called for my accounts. From these I found that I was in debt to the amount of 17,000 roubles. Before leaving Moscow for Kiev, the Empress had sent me 15,000 roubles and a large chest of simple dresses; but it was necessary for me to be richly dressed, so that, everything reckoned, I owed 2,000 roubles, and this did not appear to me an unreasonable sum. Different causes had thrown me into these expenses.

In the first place, I had arrived in Russia very badly provided for. If I had three or four dresses in the world, it was the very outside; and this at a court where people changed their dress three times a-day. A dozen chemises constituted the whole of my linen, and I had to use my mother's sheets.

In the second place, I had been told that in Russia people liked presents; and that generosity was the best means of acquiring friends and making one's self agreeable.

Thirdly, they had placed with me the most extravagant woman in Russia, the Countess Roumianzoff, who was always surrounded with tradesmen, and constantly showing me a variety of things which she induced me to purchase, and which I often purchased merely to present them to her, as I knew she was eager to have them.

The Grand Duke also cost me not a little, for he was fond of presents.

Besides, I had found out that my mother's ill-humour was easily appeased by the present of anything that pleased her; and as she was often out of temper, and especially with me, I did not neglect this means of soothing her. Her ill-humour arose in part from her being on such a bad footing with the Empress, and from the fact that her Majesty often subjected her to annoyances and humiliations. Besides, heretofore, I had always followed her; and now she could not without displeasure see me take precedence of her. I carefully avoided doing so, whenever it was possible; but in public it could not be avoided. In general, I had made it a rule to pay her the greatest respect, and treat her with all possible deference; but it was of no use, she had always and on all occasions some disagreeable remark to make, a thing which did not do her much good or prepossess people in her favour.

The Countess Roumianzoff, by her scandals and gossippings, contributed much—as did many others—to prejudice my mother in the opinion of the Empress. That carriage for eight, during the journey to Kiev, had also much to do with this result. All the old had been excluded; all the young admitted. God only knows what was tortured out of this arrangement, harmless as it was in itself. What was most evident was, that it had displeased all those who by their rank were entitled to admission, but were, nevertheless, set aside for the sake of more amusing companions. But the real foundation of all this trouble was the exclusion of Betzky and the Troubetzkoys, in whom my mother had most confidence during the journey to Kiev. Brummer and the Countess Roumianzoff had also, no doubt, contributed to it; and the carriage for eight, into which they had not been admitted, was a source of rancour.

In the month of November, the Grand Duke took the measles, at Moscow. As I had not had them, care was taken to prevent me from catching them. Those who were about the Prince did not come near us, and all diversions ceased. As soon as the disease had passed off, and the winter fully set in, we left Moscow for St. Petersburg, in sledges; my mother and me in one, the Grand Duke and Brummer in another. We celebrated the birthday of the Empress, the 18th of December, at Tver, and the next day continued our journey. Having reached the town of Chotilovo—about midway—the Grand Duke, while in my room in the evening, became unwell. He was led to his own apartments, and put to bed. He had considerable fever during the night. At noon, the next day, my mother and I went to see him; but I had scarcely passed the threshold when Count Brummer advanced towards me, and desired me not to proceed farther. I asked the reason, and learnt that indications of small-pox had just manifested themselves. As I had not had the disease, my mother instantly hurried me out of the room; and it was decided that she and I should set off the same day for St. Petersburg, leaving the Duke and his suite at Chotilovo. The Countess Roumianzoff and the lady in attendance on my mother remained there also, to nurse the invalid, they said.

A courier, despatched to the Empress, had already preceded us, and was by this time at St. Petersburg. At some distance from Novogorod, we met the Empress herself, who, having learnt that the Grand Duke had taken the small-pox, was on her way from St. Petersburg to Chotilovo, where she remained as long as the disease lasted. As soon as she perceived us, though it was in the middle of the night, she stopped her sledge and ours to make inquiries concerning the condition of the Duke. My mother told her all she knew, and she then bade the driver proceed, while we continued our journey, and reached Novogorod towards morning.

It was a Sunday, and I went to mass, after which we dined; and just as we were about to start again, the Chamberlain, Prince Galitzine, and the Gentleman of the Bedchamber, Zachar Czernicheff, arrived from Moscow, on their way to St. Petersburg. My mother was angry with the Prince because he was in company with Count Czernicheff, who had told some falsehood or other. She maintained that he ought to be avoided as a dangerous character, who indulged in gratuitous fabrications. She sulked with them both; but as this sulking was dreadfully wearisome, as, besides, there was no choice in the matter, and as these two gentlemen were better informed and had more conversational powers than any of the others, I did not join in these sulks, and this drew upon me some unpleasant remarks from my mother. At last we reached St. Petersburg, and took up our residence in one of the houses attached to the court. The palace, at that time, was not sufficiently large to allow even the Grand Duke to reside there, so that he occupied a house situated between the palace and ours. My apartments were at the left of the palace, my mother's at the right. As soon as she saw this arrangement, she became angry: first, because she thought my rooms better situated than her own; secondly, because hers were separated from mine by a common hall. In point of fact, we each had four rooms, two in front and two facing the court-yard of the house. The rooms were equal in size, and furnished exactly alike, the furniture being blue and red. But what chiefly contributed to annoy my mother was the circumstance which I am going to mention. While we were at Moscow, the Countess Roumianzoff had brought me the plan of this house by direction of the Empress, forbidding me, in her name, to speak of the matter, and consulting me as to how my mother and myself should be respectively placed. There was no choice in the case, for the two sets of apartments were in all respects equal. I said so to the Countess, and she gave me to understand that the Empress preferred my having separate rooms to occupying, as at Moscow, the same apartments as my mother. This change pleased me also, for I was much inconvenienced in being with my mother, and, in fact, no one liked the arrangement. My mother in some way got to hear of the plan that had been shown me. She spoke to me on the subject, and I told the simple truth, just as the matter had occurred. She scolded me for the secrecy I had maintained. I said I had been forbidden to speak; but she would not admit the validity of this reason, and altogether I saw that from day to day, she became more and more displeased with me, and, in fact, she had managed to quarrel with almost every one, so that she now scarcely ever came to table, either for dinner or supper, but was served in her own room. As for me, I went to her apartments three or four times a-day. The rest of my time was spent in learning Russian, in playing on the harpsichord, and in reading, for I had bought myself books; so that at fifteen I was retired, and tolerably studious for my age.

Towards the close of our stay at Moscow, a Swedish embassy arrived, at the head of which was the Senator Cedercreutz. A short time afterwards, the Count Gyllenburg also arrived, to announce to the Empress the marriage of the Prince of Sweden, my mother's brother, with a Swedish princess. Count Gyllenburg, and many other Swedes, became known to us at the time of the Prince Royal's departure for Sweden. He was a man of talent, no longer young, and my mother thought very highly of him. For myself, I was, in some respects, under obligations to him; for at Hamburg, seeing that my mother made little or no account of me, he told her she was wrong, and assured her that I was a child much beyond my age. On his arrival at St. Petersburg, he visited us, and as he had told me, while at Hamburg, that I had a very philosophical turn of mind, he asked me how it fared with my philosophy in the vortex in which I was placed. I told him how I passed my time in my room. He replied that a philosopher of fifteen could not know herself, and that I was surrounded by so many rocks that I ran great danger of being wrecked, unless the temper of my mind was of a very superior stamp; that I ought, therefore, to fortify it by the study of the best works, such as the Lives of Plutarch, that of Cicero, and the Causes of the Greatness and Decay of the Roman Republic, by Montesquieu. I immediately ordered those books to be procured for me, and there was considerable difficulty in finding them in St. Petersburg at that period. I told the Count that I would trace my portrait for him, such as I supposed it, that he might see whether or not I really did understand myself.

I did, in fact, trace out this portrait in writing, and gave it to him under the following title:—"A Portrait of the Philosopher of Fifteen." Many years afterwards, viz., in the year 1758, I turned up this portrait; and I was astonished at the accuracy and depth of self-knowledge which it evinced. Unfortunately I burnt it that same year, with all my other papers, fearing to keep a single one in my room, at the time of the unfortunate affair of Bestoujeff.

Count Gyllenburg returned my manuscript a few days afterwards. I do not know whether he took a copy. He accompanied it by some dozen pages of reflections which he had made relative to me. In these he endeavoured to strengthen my character in firmness and elevation of mind, as well as in all the other qualities of the head and heart. I read his remarks again and again, many times. I impressed them on my mind, and determined very sincerely to follow his advice. I made a promise to myself that I would do so, and when once I have made a promise to myself, I do not remember ever having failed in keeping it. Finally, I returned the manuscript to the Count as he had requested, and I confess that it has been of great service to me in forming and strengthening my mind and character.

In the beginning of February, the Empress returned from Chotilovo with the Grand Duke. As soon as we had heard of her arrival we went to receive her, and met her in the great hall, between four and five o'clock in the evening, when it was nearly dark. Notwithstanding the obscurity, however, I was almost terrified at beholding the Grand Duke. He had grown very much, but his features were scarcely to be recognized; they had all enlarged; the whole face was still swelled, and it was quite evident that he would remain deeply marked. As his hair had been cut off, he wore an immense wig, which greatly added to his disfigurement. He came to me, and asked if I did not find it difficult to recognize him. I stammered out my congratulations upon his convalescence, but in truth he had grown frightful.

On the 9th of February, 1745, a year had passed since my arrival at the court of Russia. On the 10th, the Empress celebrated the birthday of the Grand Duke. He had now entered his seventeenth year. On this occasion, I dined with her Majesty. She dined upon the throne, and I was the only guest. The Grand Duke did not appear in public that day, nor for a long time afterwards; they were in no hurry to show him in the condition in which the small-pox had left him. The Empress was very gracious during dinner. She told me that the letters I had written to her in Russian, while she was at Chotilovo, had very much pleased her (to tell the truth, they were the composition of M. Adadourof, though I had copied them out;) and she also said she had been informed that I took great pains to acquire the language of the country. She spoke to me in Russian, and wished me to reply to her in that language, which I did; and then she was pleased to praise my correct pronunciation. Finally, she told me that I had grown handsomer since my illness at Moscow. In fact, during the whole time of dinner, she was occupied in giving me marks of her kindness and affection. I returned home highly delighted with my dinner, and received congratulations on all sides. The Empress had my portrait, which the painter Caravaque had commenced, brought to her, and she kept it in her own room. It is the one which the sculptor Falconnet has carried with him to France. At the time, it was a speaking likeness.

In going to mass, or to the Empress, my mother and I had to pass through the apartments of the Grand Duke, which were situated near mine; we therefore often saw him. He also was in the habit of coming of an evening, to pass some moments with me; but there was no eagerness in these visits. On the contrary, he was always glad of any excuse for dispensing with them, and remaining at home, occupied with the childish amusements already mentioned.

A short time after the arrival of the Empress and Grand Duke at St. Petersburg, my mother met with a serious annoyance, which she could not conceal.

Prince Augustus, her brother, had written to her at Kiev, expressing his great desire to visit Russia. She had learnt that the only object of this journey was to have the administration of the territory of Holstein conferred upon him as soon as the Grand Duke became of age; and it was proposed to advance the period of his majority. In other words, it was wished to take the guardianship out of the hands of the elder brother, now become Prince Royal of Sweden, in order to give the administration of the territory of Holstein, in the name of the Grand Duke, then of age, to Prince Augustus, the younger brother of my mother and of the Prince Royal of Sweden.

This intrigue had been formed by the Holstein party, which was opposed to the Prince Royal, joined by the Danes, who could not pardon this Prince for having prevailed, in Sweden, over the Prince Royal of Denmark, whom the Dalecarlians wished to elect as successor to the throne of Sweden. My mother replied to Prince Augustus from Koselsk, telling him, that instead of lending himself to intrigues directed against his brother, it would be better for him to enter the service of Holland, where he was, and die with honour, rather than cabal against his brother and join the enemies of his sister in Russia. My mother had here reference to Count Bestoujeff, who encouraged all this intrigue in order to injure Brummer, and all the other friends of the Prince Royal of Sweden, the guardian of the Grand Duke for Holstein. This letter was opened, and read by the Count and the Empress, who was by no means pleased with my mother, and very much irritated against the Prince Royal of Sweden, who, led by his wife, sister of the King of Prussia, had allowed himself to be carried away by the French party in all their views, a party in every way opposed to Russia. He was accused of ingratitude, and my mother of want of affection for her younger brother, because she had told him to die (*se faire tuer*), an expression which was treated as harsh and inhuman; while my mother, in the company of her friends, boasted of having used a firm and sounding phrase. The result of all this was, that without any regard for my mother's feelings, or rather to mortify her and annoy the Holstein-Swedish party, Count Bestoujeff obtained permission, unknown to my mother, for Prince Augustus of Holstein to visit St. Petersburg. My mother, when she learnt that he was on his way, was extremely annoyed and grieved, and received him very coldly. But he, pushed on by Bestoujeff, ran his course. The Empress was persuaded to give him a favourable reception, which she did in appearance. This, however, did not last, and could not last, for Prince Augustus was not in himself a person of any consequence. Even his external appearance was against him. He was very small, and badly made, passionate, and with but little talent, and entirely led by his followers, who were themselves quite insignificant. His stupidity, since I must speak out, very much annoyed my mother, and, altogether, his arrival nearly drove her crazy.

Count Bestoujeff, having obtained a control over the mind of the Prince by means of his followers, killed many birds with one stone. He could not be ignorant that the Grand Duke hated Brummer as much as he did himself. Prince Augustus did not like him either, because he was attached to the Prince Royal of Sweden, under pretence of relationship and as a native of Holstein. Prince Augustus ingratiated himself with the Grand Duke by constantly talking to him about Holstein and his coming majority, so that he induced him to urge his aunt and Count Bestoujeff to advance the period. To do this, however, it was necessary to have the consent of the Roman Emperor, who, at that time, was Charles VII, of the House of Bavaria. But, meantime, he died, and the matter dragged on till the election of Francis I.

As Prince Augustus had been coldly received by my mother, and, in return, manifested but little consideration for her, this circumstance also contributed to diminish the slight remains of respect which the Grand Duke entertained for her. On the other hand, both Prince Augustus and the old valet, the favourite of the Grand Duke, fearing, seemingly, my future influence, often talked to him about the manner in which he ought to treat his wife. Romberg, an old Swedish dragoon, told him that his wife dared not speak in his presence nor meddle with his affairs; and that if she only attempted to open her mouth even, he ordered her to hold her tongue; that he was master in his own house, and that it was disgraceful for a husband to allow himself to be led by his wife like a booby.

Now the Grand Duke had about as much discretion as a cannon ball, and, when his mind was full of anything, he could not rest until he had unburdened it to the persons he was in the habit of talking with, never for a moment considering to whom it was he spoke. Consequently he used to tell me all these things, with the utmost frankness, the first time he saw me afterwards. He always fancied that every one was of his opinion, and that nothing could be more reasonable than all this. I took good care not to speak of these things to any one; but they made me reflect very seriously upon the fate which awaited me. I determined to husband carefully the confidence of the Grand Duke, in order that he might at least consider me as a person of whom he felt sure, and to whom he could confide everything without the least inconvenience to himself; and in this I succeeded for a long time. Besides, I treated every one in the best way I could, and studied how to gain the friendship, or at least to lessen the enmity of those whom I in any way suspected of being badly disposed to me. I showed no leaning to any side, nor meddled with anything; always maintained a serene air, treated every one with great attention, affability, and politeness, and, as I was naturally very gay, I saw with pleasure that from day to day I advanced in the general esteem, and was looked upon as an interesting child, and one by no means wanting in mind. I showed great respect for my mother, a boundless obedience for the Empress, and the most profound deference for the Grand Duke; and I sought with the most anxious care to gain the affection of the public.

From the period of our visit to Moscow, the Empress had assigned me some ladies and gentlemen who formed my court. A short time after my arrival at St. Petersburg she gave me some Russian maids, in order, as she said, to aid me in acquiring increased facility in the use of the language. This arrangement pleased me very much; for these persons were all young, the oldest of them being only about twenty; all, too, were very lively, so that from that time I did nothing but sing, dance, and play in my room, from the moment I awoke in the morning till I went to sleep again at night. In the evening, after supper, I brought into my bed-room my three maids, the two Princesses Gagarine and Mademoiselle Koucheleff, and we played at blind-man's buff and all sorts of games suited to our age. All these ladies mortally feared the Countess Roumianzoff; but as she played at cards from morning till night, either in the ante-chamber or in her own room, never leaving her chair, except from necessity, she rarely came near us.

In the midst of our mirth, the fancy seized me to distribute among my women the care of all my effects. I placed my money, my expenditure, and my linen in the charge of Mademoiselle Schenck, the lady's-maid whom I had brought from Germany; she was a silly and querulous old maid, to whom our gaiety was extremely annoying; and besides that, she was jealous of all these young companions who were about to share her functions and my affection. I gave all my jewels to Mademoiselle Joukoff; she having more intelligence and being more gay and frank than the others, began to gain my favour. My clothes I entrusted to my valet Timothy Yevreinoff; my lace to Mademoiselle Balkoff, who afterwards married the poet Soumarokoff; my ribbons to the elder Mademoiselle Scorochodov, since married to Aristarchus Kachkine; her younger sister Anne having nothing, as she was only between thirteen and fourteen years old.

The day after this grand arrangement, in which I had exercised my central power within the limits of my own chamber, and without consulting a living soul, there were theatricals in the evening. To go to them, it was necessary to pass through my mother's apartments. The Empress, the Grand Duke, and the whole court were there. A little theatre had been erected in a riding-school, which, in the time of the Empress Anne, had been used by the Duke of Courland, whose apartments I now occupied. After the play, when the Empress had retired, the Countess Roumianzoff came into my room, and told me that the Empress disapproved of the arrangement I had made in distributing the care of my effects among my women, and that she was ordered to withdraw the keys of my jewels out of the hands of Mademoiselle Joukoff, and restore them to Mademoiselle Schenck, which she did in my presence, and then departed, leaving Mademoiselle Joukoff and me with faces somewhat elongated, and Mademoiselle Schenck triumphing in the marked confidence of the Empress. She began to assume with me arrogant airs, which made her more ridiculous than ever, and even less amiable than she had been before.

The first week of Lent I had a singular scene with the Grand Duke. In the morning, while in my room with my maids, who were all very devout, listening to matins, which were sung in the ante-chamber, I received an embassy from the Grand Duke. He had sent me his dwarf to inquire how I was, and to tell me that, on account of its being Lent, he should not visit me that day. The dwarf found us all listening to the prayers, and fulfilling exactly the prescriptions of Lent, according to our creed. I returned the usual compliments to the Duke, through his dwarf, who then departed. When he got back, whether it was that he had really been edified by what he had seen, or that he wished his dear lord and master, who was anything but devout, to do the same, he passed a high eulogium upon the devotion which reigned in my apartments, and, by doing so, put the Duke in a very bad humour with me. The first time we met he began by sulking. Having asked the cause of this, he scolded me very much for what he called the excessive devotion to which I gave myself up. When I asked who had told him this, he named his dwarf as an eye-witness of it. I told him I did no more than was proper, only what every one else did, and what could not be dispensed with without scandal; but he thought differently. The dispute ended as most disputes do, by leaving each one with his own opinion; but, as his Imperial Highness had no one but me to speak to during mass, he gradually left off pouting.

Two days after, I had another alarm. In the morning, while matins were being sung in my apartments, Mademoiselle Schenck entered my room in great consternation, telling me that my mother had been taken ill, and had fainted. I instantly ran to her, and found her lying on the ground on a mattress, but not unconscious. I ventured to ask her what was the matter. She told me, that wishing to be bled, the surgeon was so clumsy as to miss four times, having tried both arms and both feet, and that she had fainted. I knew that she dreaded bleeding; I was ignorant of her intention in wishing to be bled, and did not even know that she stood in need of it. Yet she reproached me with caring little for her condition, and said many disagreeable things on the subject. I excused myself in the best way I could, acknowledging my ignorance; but, seeing that she was in a very bad humour, I became silent, and endeavoured to restrain my tears, nor did I leave her till she had desired me to do so with some degree of harshness. On my return to my room, in tears, my maids wanted to know what was the matter, and I told them quite simply. I went several times during the day to my mother's room, and remained there as long as I thought I could do so without being troublesome. This was a capital point with her, to which I was so well accustomed, that there is nothing I have so carefully avoided during my life as remaining with any one longer than I was wanted. I have made it a point instantly to retire whenever the least suspicion crossed my mind that my farther stay would be an inconvenience. But I know by experience that every one does not act upon the same principle, for my own patience has often been put to the test by those who do not know how to go away before they have worn out their welcome or become a source of weariness.

In the course of the Lent, my mother had a grief which was very real. At a time when it was least expected, she received the news of the sudden death of my younger sister, Elizabeth, a child only between three and four years old. She was very much afflicted, and I grieved also.

One morning, some few days afterwards, I saw the Empress come into my room. She sent for my mother, and they retired to my dressing-room, where they had a long and private conversation; after which they returned into my bed-room, and I saw that my mother's eyes were red and filled with tears. From the sequence of the conversation I understood that they had been talking about the death of the Emperor Charles VII, of the house of Bavaria, the news of which had just reached the Empress. Her Majesty was then without alliance, and she hesitated between Prussia and the house of Austria, each of which had their partisans. She had the same complaint against Austria as against France, towards which the King of Prussia leaned, for the Marquis de Botta, the minister of the court of Vienna had been sent away from Russia for speaking against the Empress—an act which at the time it was sought to represent as a conspiracy. The Marquis de la Chétardie had been similarly dismissed for the same reasons. I do not know what was the object of this conversation, but my mother seemed to conceive great hopes from it, and went away very well satisfied. As for me, I was in all this simply a spectator, and one, too, very passive, very discreet, and pretty nearly indifferent.

After Easter, when the spring had fully set in, I expressed to the Countess Roumianzoff the desire I had to learn to ride, and she obtained the consent of the Empress. I had begun to have pains in the chest at the commencement of the year, after the pleurisy I had had in Moscow, and I was still very thin. The doctors ordered me milk and Seltzer water every morning. It was at Roumianzoff House, in the barracks of the Ismaïlofsky regiment, that I took my first lesson in riding. I had already ridden several times at Moscow, but very badly.

In the month of May, the Empress, with the Grand Duke, went to occupy the Summer Palace. To my mother and I had been assigned a stone building, by the side of the Fontanka, close to the house of Peter I. My mother occupied one side of this building, and I the other. Here ended all the assiduities of the Grand Duke; he told me quite plainly, and through a servant, that he now lived too far off to come and see me often. I fully perceived his want of interest, and how little I was cared for. My self-esteem and vanity grieved in silence, but I was too proud to complain. I should have thought myself degraded if any one had shown me a friendship which I could have taken for pity. Nevertheless, I shed tears when alone, then quietly dried them up, and went to romp with my maids. My mother also treated me with great coldness and ceremony, but I never missed visiting her several times during the day. At heart I felt very sad, but I took care not to speak of this. However, Mademoiselle Joukoff one day perceived my tears, and spoke to me on the subject. I gave her the best reasons I could, without however giving her the true ones. I laboured more earnestly than before to gain the affection of every one. Great or small, I neglected no one, but laid it down to myself as a rule to believe that I stood in need of every one, and so to act in consequence as to obtain the good will of all; and I succeeded in doing so.

After some days' stay in the Summer Palace, where people began to speak of the preparations for my marriage, the court removed to Peterhoff, where it was more concentrated than in the city. The Empress and the Grand Duke occupied the upper portion of the house built by Peter I; my mother and I were beneath, in the apartments of the Grand Duke. We dined with him every day, under a tent, upon the open gallery adjoining his apartments; he supped with us. The Empress was often absent, moving about among her different country residences. We were out a good deal, walking, riding, or driving. I then saw as clear as day, that the persons about the Grand Duke had lost all credit with him, and all control over him. The military games, which he formerly carried on in private, he now enacted almost in their presence. Count Brummer and his head master scarcely ever saw him, except to follow him in public. The rest of his time was literally passed, in the company of his valets, in acts of childishness unheard of at his age, for he played at puppets.

My mother took advantage of the absences of the Empress to go and sup at the neighbouring mansions, and especially at that of the Prince and Princess of Hesse-Homburg. One evening when she had ridden out there, I was sitting, after supper, in my room, which was on a level with the garden, one of the doors leading into it, when I felt tempted by the fine weather. I proposed to my maids and my three ladies of honour to take a walk in the garden; and I had no great trouble in persuading them. We were eight, and my valet, who made nine, followed us with two other valets. We walked about till midnight in the most innocent manner possible. My mother having returned, Mademoiselle Schenck, who had refused to accompany us, and grumbled at our project, was in a great hurry to tell her that I had gone out against her advice. My mother went to bed, and when I got back with my troop, Mademoiselle Schenck told me, with an air of triumph, that my mother had sent twice to inquire if I had returned, as she wished to speak to me; but that as it was very late, and she tired of waiting, she had gone to bed. I would have instantly gone to her, but I found the door closed. I told Schenck that she might have had me called. She pretended that she had not been able to find us; but this was a mere story to make a quarrel, and get me scolded; I saw this clearly, and went to bed with a good deal of uneasiness. The following day, as soon as I awoke, I went to my mother and found her in bed. I approached to kiss her hand, but she angrily withdrew it, and gave me a dreadful scolding for having dared to walk out at night without her permission. I said she was not at home; but she replied that the hour was improper, and said all sorts of disagreeable things, for the purpose, seemingly, of giving me a distaste for nocturnal promenades. This, however, is certain, that although this walk may have been an imprudence, nothing could have been more innocent. What most distressed me was, that she accused me of having gone up to the apartments of the Grand Duke. I replied that this was an abominable calumny, at which she became so enraged that she seemed out of herself. It was in vain that I went on my knees to soothe her irritation. She treated my submission as acting, and ordered me out of the room. I retired to my own apartments in tears. At dinner-time I ascended with her, she still being very angry, to the apartments of the Grand Duke, who inquired what was the matter, as my eyes were very red. I told him exactly what had happened. This time he took my part, and accused my mother of being capricious and passionate. I begged him not to speak to her on the subject, which request he complied with, and by degrees her anger wore off; but I was always treated very coldly. We left Peterhoff at the end of July, and returned to the city, where all was preparation for the approaching marriage.

At last the Empress fixed the 21st of August for the ceremony. As the day came nearer, I became more and more melancholy. My heart predicted but little happiness; ambition alone sustained me. In my inmost soul there was a something which never allowed me to doubt for a single moment that sooner or later I should become the sovereign Empress of Russia in my own right.

The marriage was celebrated with much pomp and magnificence. In the evening I found in my room Madame Krause, sister of the head lady's-maid to the Empress, who had placed her with me as my head lady's-maid. From the very next day I found that this person had thrown all my other women into consternation, for on approaching one of them to speak to her, as usual, she said to me, "In God's name, do not come near me; we have been forbidden to whisper to you." On the other hand, my beloved spouse did not trouble himself in the slightest degree about me, but was constantly with his valets, playing at soldiers, exercising them in his room, or changing his uniform twenty times a-day. I yawned, and grew weary, having no one to speak to; or I endeavoured to keep up appearances. On the third day after my marriage, the Countess Roumianzoff Sent me word that the Empress had dispensed with her attendance on me, and that she was going to return home to her husband and children. This did not grieve me much, for she had been the cause of a great deal of scandal.

The marriage festivities lasted ten days, at the end of which the Grand Duke and myself took up our residence in the Summer Palace, where the Empress was living; and the departure of my mother was beginning to be talked of. Since my marriage I did not see her every day; but she had very much softened towards me. About the latter end of September she took her departure, the Grand Duke and I accompanying her as far as Krasnoe-Selo. I was sincerely afflicted, and wept a great deal. After taking leave of her we returned to the city. On reaching the palace I called for Mademoiselle Joukoff. I was told that she had gone to see her mother who was ill. The next day I put the same question, and received the same answer. About noon the Empress passed with great pomp from the Summer to the Winter Palace. We followed her to her apartments. Having reached the state bed-room she stopped, and, after some casual remarks, spoke of my mother's departure, and told me, with apparent kindness, to moderate my grief. But I thought I should have dropped when she said, in the presence of some thirty people, that at my mother's request she had dismissed from my service Mademoiselle Joukoff, because my mother feared I might become too much attached to a person who so little deserved my favour; and then her Majesty spoke very pointedly against the poor girl. I certainly was no way edified with this scene, nor convinced of what her Majesty advanced; but I was deeply afflicted at the misfortune of poor Joukoff, dismissed from court solely because, from her sociable disposition, she suited me better than my other women. "For why," as I said to myself, "was she placed with me if she was not worthy?" My mother could not know her, could not even speak to her, as she did not understand Russian, the only language with which Joukoff was acquainted; she could only have been guided by the silly remarks of Schenck, who scarcely possessed common sense. This girl suffers for me, I said to myself; I must not, therefore, abandon her in her misfortune, of which my affection has been the sole cause. I have never been able to learn whether or not my mother really had requested the Empress to dismiss this person from my service; if so, she must have preferred violent measures to those of mildness, for she never opened her lips to me in reference to the girl; and yet a single word from her would have been sufficient to put me on my guard, at least, against an attachment in itself very innocent. The Empress, also, might have acted with less austerity. The girl was young: it was only necessary to have found a suitable match for her, which might easily have been done; but instead of this they acted in the manner I have mentioned.

The Empress having dismissed us, the Grand Duke and I proceeded to our own apartments. On our way, I perceived that her Majesty had already acquainted her nephew with what she had done. I stated to him my objections on the subject, and made him understand that this girl was unfortunate solely because it was supposed that I had a liking for her; and that since she was suffering on account of my affection, I thought myself justified in not abandoning her, as far, at all events, as depended on myself. In fact, I immediately sent her some money, through my valet; but he informed me that she had already departed for Moscow with her mother and sister. I ordered what I had destined for her to be sent through her brother, who was a sergeant in the guards. I learnt that he also, together with his wife, had been ordered away, and that he had been placed as an officer in a country regiment. At the present time I am scarcely able to give any plausible explanation of these things; it seems to me like doing wrong gratis, and from mere caprice, without a shadow of reason, or even of pretext. But matters did not stop even here. Through my valet and my other attendants, I endeavoured to find for Mademoiselle Joukoff a suitable match. One was proposed to me: it was a sergeant in the guards, a gentleman of some property, named Travin. He went to Moscow to marry her, provided she suited him. He did marry her, and was made lieutenant in a country regiment. As soon as the Empress heard of this, she banished them both to Astracan. It is difficult to find a reason for such persecution.

At the Winter Palace, the Grand Duke and I occupied the apartments which we had previously used; those of the Duke were separated from mine by an immense staircase, which also led to the apartments of the Empress. In going to him, or in his coming to me, it was necessary to cross the landing of this staircase—not the pleasantest thing in the world, especially in winter. Nevertheless, we made the passage several times a-day. In the evening, I went to play at billiards in his ante-chamber with the Chamberlain Berkholz, while he romped with his gentlemen in the other room. My party at billiards was interrupted by the retirement of Brummer and Berkholz, whom the Empress dismissed from attendance on the Grand Duke, at the end of the winter of 1746. This winter was passed in masquerades given at the principal houses in the city, which were then very small. The court and the whole town assisted at them regularly. The last of them was given by the Master-General of the Police, Tatizcheff, in a house called Smolnoy Dvoretz, belonging to the Empress. The centre portion of this wooden house had been destroyed by a fire; nothing remained but the wings, which were of two stories. One of these wings was set apart for dancing; but in order to go to supper, which was laid out in the other, it was necessary to pass, and this in the month of January, through the court-yard and the snow. After supper this journey had to be repeated. The Grand Duke returned home, and went to bed, but the next morning he awoke with a violent headache, which prevented him from rising. I sent for the doctors, who pronounced him in a burning fever of the most violent kind. He was carried in the evening from my bed to the audience-chamber, where, after being bled, he was placed in a bed arranged there for him. They bled him several times; he was very ill. The Empress visited him frequently during the day, and seeing me in tears, she was pleased with me. One evening, while reading the night-prayers in a small oratory adjoining my dressing-room, Madame Ismaïloff came in. She was a person of whom the Empress was very fond, and she informed me that her Majesty, knowing I was much afflicted by the illness of the Duke, had sent her to tell me not to be cast down, but to put my trust in God, and that whatever happened she would not forsake me. She then asked me what I was reading; I told her the prayers for night, and she said I should hurt my eyes by reading such small print by candle-light. I then begged her to thank her Imperial Majesty for her goodness towards me, and we parted very affectionately, she to give an account of her mission, I to go to bed. Next day the Empress sent me a prayer-book printed in large type, in order to preserve my eyes, she said. Although the room in which the Grand Duke was placed adjoined mine, I never entered it except when I felt that I should not be in the way, for I saw that he did not care much to have me there, but preferred being with his attendants, who, on the other hand, did not much suit me. Besides, I was not much accustomed to pass my time alone among a set of men. Meanwhile, Lent came round. I went to my duty (*fis mes dévotions*) the first week. Generally speaking, I was inclined to devotion at that period. I saw plainly that the Grand Duke cared little about me. A fortnight after our marriage he confessed to me again that he was in love with Mademoiselle Carr, Maid of Honour to her Imperial Majesty, since married to a Prince Galitzine, Equery to the Empress. He told Count Devier, his Chamberlain, that there was no comparison between that lady and me. Devier maintained the contrary, and the Duke got angry with him. This scene took place almost in my presence, and I witnessed their contest. Surely, I said to myself, it would be impossible for me not to be unhappy with such a man as this, were I to give way to sentiments of tenderness thus requited. I might die of jealousy without benefit to any one. I endeavoured therefore to master my feelings, so as not to be jealous of a man who did not love me. Had he wished to be loved, I should have found no difficulty in loving him. I was naturally well disposed, and accustomed to fulfil my duties; but then, too, I should have required a husband who had common sense, which this one had not.

I had abstained (*fait maigre*) during the first week of Lent. On the Saturday, the Empress sent me word that it would give her pleasure if I abstained during the second week also. I replied that I begged her Majesty would permit me to abstain during the entire Lent. Sievers, Marshal of the Court to the Empress, a son-in-law to Madame Krause, who was the bearer of this message, told me that the Empress was greatly pleased with my request, and that she granted it. When the Grand Duke learned that I continued to abstain, he scolded me a good deal; but I told him I could not do otherwise. After he had got well, he still feigned illness in order not to leave his room, where he found more congenial amusement than in the formal life of the court. He did not quit it till the last week of Lent, when he went to his duty.

After Easter, he had a marionette theatre set up in his room, and invited company to see it, and even ladies. This show was the most insipid thing imaginable. The room in which it was set up had a door which was fastened up, in consequence of its leading into one of the Empress' apartments. In this apartment there was a mechanical table, which could be lowered and raised so as to admit of dining without servants. One day, while the Grand Duke was in his room preparing his so-called theatricals, he heard people talking in this room beyond, and, with his usual inconsiderate vivacity, he took up from his theatre one of those carpenters' tools used for making holes in boards, and set to work boring holes in this condemned door, so that he could see all that passed within, and among other things, the dinner which the Empress was then taking there. The Master of the Hounds, Count Razoumowsky, in a brocaded dressing-gown, dined with her—he had taken medicine that day—and there were, besides, some dozen persons of those most in the confidence of the Empress. The Grand Duke, not content with enjoying the fruit of his skilful labour himself, must needs call all who were about him to share in the pleasure of looking through the holes which he had bored with so much diligence. When all were fully satisfied with this indiscreet pleasure, he came and invited Madame Krause, myself, and my maids, to go to his room and see something which we had never seen before. He did not tell us what it was, doubtless to give us an agreeable surprise. As I did not hurry myself sufficiently to gratify his impatience, he led away Madame Krause and my women. I arrived last, and found them stationed in front of this door, where he had placed benches, chairs, and stools, for the accommodation of the spectators, as he said. On entering, I asked what all this was about. He ran to meet me, and told me what the case was. I was terrified and indignant at his rashness, and told him I would neither look nor have anything to do with this impropriety, which would certainly bring him into trouble if his aunt should come to hear of it, and this she could not well help doing, seeing that there were at least twenty persons in his secret. All who had allowed themselves to look through the door, finding that I would not do the same, began to file off one after the other. The Duke himself became ashamed of what he had done, and recommenced working on his theatre. I returned to my room.

Up to the Sunday, we heard nothing of this affair; but on that day it happened, I hardly know how, that I got to mass rather later than usual. On returning to my room, I was about taking off my court dress, when I saw the Empress enter with a flushed and angry look. As she had not been at the chapel mass, but had heard mass in her private oratory, I went to meet her, to kiss her hand as usual, as I had not seen her before that day. She kissed me, desired the Grand Duke to be sent for, and, while waiting for him, scolded me for being late at mass, and preferring my own adornment to the service of God. She added that in the time of the Empress Anne, though not living at court, but in a house at some distance from the palace, she had never failed in her duties, but often got up by candle-light for this purpose. Then she sent for the valet de chambre who dressed my hair, and told him that for the future, if he was so slow in dressing my hair, she would have him dismissed. When she had ended with him, the Grand Duke, who had undressed in his own room, entered in his dressing-gown, with his night cap in his hand, and with a gay and careless air. He ran to kiss the hand of the Empress, who embraced him, and then asked him how he had dared to act in the manner he had done, adding that she had gone into the room which contained the mechanical table, and found the door all pierced with holes, all these holes being directed towards the place where she usually sat; that he seemed to have forgotten what he owed her; that she could no longer consider him as anything but an ungrateful person; that her father, Peter I., had also an ungrateful son, and that he punished him by disinheriting him; that, in the time of the Empress Anne, she had never failed in giving her the respect due to a crowned head, anointed of the Lord; that the Empress Anne did not understand jokes, but sent to the Fortress those who were wanting in respect; that as for him, he was but a little boy, and she would teach him how to behave. At this he began to get angry, and would have answered her, stammering out a few words to this effect, but she commanded him to be silent, and became so excited that her anger knew no bounds, as was usually the case when she got into a passion. She loaded him with insults, and said all sorts of shocking things, treating him with as much contempt as anger.

We were thunderstruck, and although this scene did not refer directly to me, yet tears came into my eyes. She perceived this, and said to me, "This does not apply to you; I know that you had nothing to do with this act, and that you neither looked nor wished to look through the door." This remark, which was correct, calmed her a little, and she stopped; besides, it would have been difficult for her to have gone farther than she had done. She then wished us good morning, and retired, with a flushed face and flashing eyes. The Grand Duke went to his room, and I undressed in silence, ruminating on what I had heard. When I had done, the Duke returned, and said to me—in a tone half sheepish, half comical—"She was like a fury, and did not know what she said." "She was dreadfully angry," I replied. We talked over the matter, and then dined in my room, quite alone. When the Grand Duke had gone to his own apartments, Madame Krause entered my room. "It must be acknowledged," she said, "that the Empress has acted like a true mother to-day." I saw she wished to make me talk, and therefore I said nothing. She continued: "A mother gets angry, scolds her children, and there the matter ends; you ought both of you to have said to her, *I beg your pardon, Madame*, and you would have disarmed her." I said I was astounded and petrified by her Majesty's anger, and all I could do at the moment was to listen and be silent. She then left me, probably to make her report. As for me, the "*I beg your pardon, Madame*," as a means of disarming the anger of the Empress, remained in my head; and I have since used it with success, when occasion required, as will be seen in the sequel.

Some time before the Empress had relieved Count Brummer and the Great Chamberlain from attendance on the Grand Duke, I happened one day to go earlier than usual into the ante-chamber. The Count was there alone, and seized the occasion to speak to me. He begged and entreated me to go every day to the Empress' dressing-room, as my mother, at leaving, had obtained permission for me to do; a privilege of which I had made very little use hitherto, as it was a prerogative which wearied me excessively. I had gone once or twice, and found there the Empress' women, who retired by degrees, so that I was left alone. I told him this. He said it was of no consequence, I ought to continue. But I could not understand this courtier-like perseverance. It might answer his views, but it did not at all suit me to be kept standing in the Empress' dressing-room, and be, besides, an inconvenience to her. I stated to him my repugnance, but he did everything to persuade me, though without success. I was much better pleased to be in my own rooms, especially when Madame Krause was not there. I had discovered in her this winter a very decided propensity for drink, and as she soon after got her daughter married to the Marshal of the Court, Sievers, she either was out a good deal, or my people contrived to make her tipsy, when she went to sleep, and my room was delivered from this surly Argus.

Count Brummer and the Grand Chamberlain Berkholz having been relieved from their duties about the Prince, the Empress named as his attendant General Prince Basil Repnine. A better appointment could not have been made, for Prince Repnine was not only a man of honour and probity, he was also a man of talent, a very worthy man, candid and straightforward. For my own-self, I had every reason to be satisfied with the conduct of Prince Repnine. For Count Brummer I felt no regret; he wearied me with his eternal politics, he smelt of intrigue; while the frank and soldier-like character of Prince Repnine inspired me with confidence. As for the Grand Duke, he was delighted to get rid of his pedagogues, whom he hated. In quitting him, however, they left him with no slight anxiety at finding himself at the mercy of the intrigues of Count Bestoujeff, who was the prime mover in all these changes, made under the plausible pretext of the majority of his Imperial Highness in his duchy of Holstein. Prince Augustus, my uncle, was still at St. Petersburg, watching the administration of the Grand Duke's hereditary territory.

In the month of May we moved to the Summer Palace. At the end of the month the Empress placed with me, as chief housekeeper, Madame Tchoglokoff, one of her maids of honour, and her relative. This was a thunderbolt for me. This lady was altogether in the interest of Count Bestoujeff, extremely silly, spiteful, capricious, and very selfish. Her husband, Chamberlain to the Empress, was then gone on some sort of mission from her Majesty to Vienna. I wept a great deal on seeing her arrive, and all the rest of the day. I was to be bled on the following day. In the morning the Empress came to my room, and seeing my eyes red, said to me that young women who did not love their husbands were always crying; that my mother, however, had assured her I had no repugnance to marrying the Grand Duke; that, besides, she had not forced me; that, as I was married, I must not cry any more. I remembered the instructions of Madame Krause, and said to her, *I beg your pardon, Madame*, and she was appeased. Meanwhile the Grand Duke came in, and this time the Empress received him very graciously, and then went away. I was bled, and indeed I required it; I then went to bed, and wept the whole day. The next day, the Grand Duke drew me aside in the course of the afternoon, and I saw clearly that they had given him to understand that Madame Tchoglokoff had been placed with me because I did not love him. But I cannot understand how they expected to increase my attachment for him by giving me that woman; and so I told him. As to placing her with me as an Argus, that was a different matter. But if this was their object, they ought to have chosen some one less stupid; and, besides, it was not necessary for this purpose to be spiteful and malevolent. Madame Tchoglokoff was thought to be extremely virtuous, because she loved her husband to adoration. She had married him for love: so excellent an example placed before me would perhaps persuade me to imitate it. We shall see how far the experiment was successful. In all probability, it was the circumstance which I am about to relate which precipitated this arrangement. I say precipitated, because I believe that, from the beginning, Count Bestoujeff had it in view to surround us with his creatures. He would gladly have done the same in the case of the Empress also, but that was not so easy.

The Grand Duke, at the time I arrived in Moscow, had in his service three domestics named Czernicheff, all three sons of grenadiers in the bodyguard of the Empress. Their fathers held the rank of lieutenant, which they received as a recompense for having aided in placing the Empress on the throne. The oldest of the Czernicheffs was cousin to the two others, who were brothers. The Grand Duke was very fond of all three. They were the persons most in his confidence, and were really very useful. All three were tall and well made, especially the oldest. The Duke made use of him in all his commissions, and several times in the day he sent him to me. He it was, too, whom the Duke made his confidant when he did not care to come to me. This man was on very intimate and friendly terms with my valet Yevreinoff, and through this channel I often knew things which I should otherwise have been ignorant of. Besides, both of them were attached to me heart and soul, and I often obtained information from them, on a variety of matters, which it would have been difficult to have procured otherwise. I do not know in reference to what it was that the oldest of the Czernicheffs said one day to the Grand Duke, "she is not my intended, but yours." This expression made the Grand Duke laugh. He related it to me, and from that time it pleased his Imperial Highness, when speaking to me, to call me his intended, and Andrew Czernicheff your intended. After our marriage Andrew Czernicheff, to put a stop to this badinage, proposed to his Imperial Highness to call me his mother, and I, on my part, called him my son. Now between the Grand Duke and myself there was always some reference to this son, for he was excessively attached to the man; and I also liked him very much.

My servants were greatly disturbed on this account; some through jealousy, others from apprehension of the consequences which might result both for them and for us. One day when there was a masked ball at court, and I had gone to my room to change my dress, my valet Timothy Yevreinoff took me aside, and told me that he and all my servants were terrified at the danger into which he saw me plunging. I asked him what he meant. He said, "You speak of nothing and think of nothing but Andrew Czernicheff." "Well," I said, in the innocence of my heart, "what harm is there in that? He is my son. The Grand Duke likes him as much and more than I do; and he is devoted and faithful to us." "Yes," he replied, "that is all very true; the Grand Duke can do as he pleases; but you have not the same right. What you call kindness and attachment, because this man is faithful and serves you, your people call love." The utterance of this word, which had never once occurred to me, was a thunderbolt; first, on account of the opinion of my servants, which I called rash; secondly, on account of the condition in which I had placed myself, without being aware of it. He told me that he had advised his friend Czernicheff to pretend illness in order to put an end to these remarks. This advice Czernicheff followed, and his feigned illness lasted pretty nearly to the month of April. The Grand Duke was much concerned about him, and spoke of him continually to me. He had not the slightest suspicion of the real circumstances. At the Summer Palace Andrew Czernicheff again made his appearance. I could no longer meet him without embarrassment. Meanwhile the Empress had thought proper to make a new arrangement with the servants of the court. They were to serve in turn in all the rooms, and Andrew Czernicheff like the rest. The Grand Duke often had concerts in the afternoon, and he himself played the violin at them. During one of these concerts, which usually wearied me, I went to my own room. This opened into the great hall of the Summer Palace, which was then filled with scaffoldings, as they were painting the ceiling. The Empress was absent; Madame Krause had gone to her daughter's, Madame Sievers; and I did not find a soul in my room. From *ennui* I opened the door of the hall, and saw at the other end Andrew Czernicheff. I made a sign to him to approach; he came to the door, though with much apprehension. I asked him if the Empress would return soon. He said, "I cannot speak to you; they make too much noise in the hall; let me come into your room." I replied, "That I will not do." He was outside the door and I within, holding the door half open as I spoke to him. An involuntary impulse made me turn my head in the direction opposite to the door at which I stood, and I saw behind me at the other door of my dressing-room, the Chamberlain, Count Divier, who said to me, "The Grand Duke wishes to see you, madam." I closed the door of the hall, and returned with Count Divier to the apartment where the Grand Duke was giving his concert. I have since learnt that Count

Catherine II of Russia in a portrait by Vigilius Eriksen in 1762

Divier was a kind of reporter employed as such, like many others about me. The following day, which was Sunday, after mass, we learnt—that is, the Grand Duke and I—that the three Czernicheffs had been placed as lieutenants in the regiments stationed near Orenburg; and in the afternoon of this day Madame Tchoglokoff was placed with me.

A few days afterwards, we received orders to prepare to accompany the Empress to Reval. At the same time, Madame Tchoglokoff told me from her Majesty that, for the future, her Imperial Majesty would dispense with my coming to her dressing-room, and that if I had any communication to make to her it must not be made through any one but Madame Tchoglokoff. In my own mind, I was delighted with this order, which relieved me from the necessity of being kept standing among the Empress' women; besides, I seldom went to her dressing-room, and then but rarely saw her. During the whole time that I had been going there I had not seen her more than three or four times, and, generally speaking, whenever I went, her women quitted the room one after the other. Not to be left there alone, I seldom stayed long either.

In the month of June the Empress set out for Reval, and we accompanied her. The Grand Duke and I travelled in a carriage for four persons; Prince Augustus and Madame Tchoglokoff made up its complement. Our plan of travelling was neither agreeable nor convenient. The post-houses or stations were occupied by the Empress; we were accommodated in tents or in the outhouses. I remember that on one occasion, during this journey, I dressed near the oven where the bread had just been baked; and that another time, when I entered the tent where my bed was placed, there was water in it up to the ankle. Besides all this, the Empress had no fixed hour, either for setting out or stopping, for meals or repose. We were all, masters and servants, strangely harassed.

After ten or twelve days' march, we reached an estate belonging to Count Steinbock, forty verstes from Reval. From this place the Empress departed in great state, wishing to reach Catherinthal in the evening; but somehow it happened that the journey was prolonged till half-past one in the morning.

During the entire journey, from St. Petersburg to Reval, Madame Tchoglokoff was the torment of our carriage. To the simplest thing that was said, she would reply, "Such a remark would displease her Majesty;" or, "Such a thing would not be approved of by her Majesty." It was sometimes to the most innocent and indifferent matters that she attached these etiquettes. As for me, I made up my mind, and during the whole journey slept continually while in the carriage. From the day after our arrival at Catherinthal, the court recommenced its ordinary round of occupations; that is to say, from morning till night, and far into the night, gambling, and for rather high stakes, was carried on in the ante-chamber of the Empress, a hall which divided the house and its two stories into two sections.

Madame Tchoglokoff was a gambler; she induced me to play at faro like the rest. All the favourites of the Empress were ordinarily fixed here when they did not happen to be in her Majesty's room, or rather tent, for she had erected a very large and magnificent tent at the side of her apartments, which were on the ground floor, and very small, as was usually the case with the structures of Peter I. He had built this country residence, and planted the garden.

The Prince and Princess Repnine, who were of the party, and were aware of the arrogant and senseless conduct of Madame Tchoglokoff during the journey, persuaded me to speak of it to the Countess Schouvaloff and Madame Ismaïloff, the ladies most in her Majesty's favour. These ladies had no love for Madame Tchoglokoff, and they had already learnt what had happened. The little Countess Schouvaloff, who was indiscretion itself, did not wait for me to speak to her, but happening to be seated by my side at play, she introduced the subject herself, and, being very humorous, she placed the whole conduct of Madame Tchoglokoff in such a ridiculous light, that she soon made her the laughing-stock of every one. She did more; she related to the Empress all that had passed. It would seem as if Madame Tchoglokoff had received a reproof, for she lowered her tone very considerably with me. Indeed, there was much need of this being done, for I began to feel a great tendency to melancholy. I felt totally isolated. The Grand Duke, at Reval, took a passing fancy for a Madame Cédéraparre. As usual, he did not fail to confide the matter to me immediately. I had frequent pains in the chest, and at Catherinthal a spitting of blood, for which I was bled. On the afternoon of that day, Madame Tchoglokoff came to my room, and found me in tears. With a countenance greatly softened, she asked me what was the matter, and proposed to me, on the part of the Empress, to take a walk in the garden, to dissipate my hopochondria, as she said. That day the Grand Duke had gone to hunt with the Master of the Hounds, Count Razoumowsky. She also placed in my hands, as a present from her Imperial Majesty, 3000 roubles, for playing at faro. The ladies had noticed that I was without money, and told the Empress. I begged Madame Tchoglokoff to thank her Majesty for her goodness, and then went with her for a walk in the garden.

Some days after our arrival at Catherinthal, the High Chancellor, Count Bestoujeff, arrived, accompanied by the

Imperial Ambassador, the Baron Preyslain, and we learned, by the tenor of his congratulations, that the two imperial courts had just become united by a treaty of alliance. In consequence of this, the Empress went to see her fleet manœuvre; but, except the smoke of the cannons, we saw nothing. The day was excessively hot, and the sea perfectly calm. On returning from this manœuvre, there was a ball in the Empress' tents, which were erected on the terrace. The supper was spread in the open air, around a basin intended for a fountain; but scarcely had her Majesty taken her seat, when there came on a shower which wetted the entire company, forcing it to disperse and seek shelter, as best it could, in the houses and in the tents. Thus ended this *fête*.

Some days afterwards the Empress departed for Roguervick. The fleet manœuvred there also, and again we saw nothing but smoke. In this journey we all suffered very much in our feet. The soil of the place is a rock, covered with a thick bed of pebbles, of such a nature that if one stood for a short time in the same spot, the feet would sink in and the pebbles cover them. We encamped here for several days, and were forced to walk, in passing from tent to tent, and in our tents, upon this ground. For more than four months afterwards my feet were sore in consequence. The convicts who worked at the pier wore sabots, and even these seldom lasted beyond eight or ten days.

The imperial ambassador had followed her Majesty to this port. He dined there and supped with her half-way between Roguervick and Reval. During this supper an old woman, who had reached the age of 130 years, was led before the Empress. She looked like a walking skeleton. The Empress sent her meat from her own table, as well as money, and we continued our journey.

On our return to Catherinthal, Madame Tchoglokoff had the satisfaction of finding there her husband, who had returned from his mission to Vienna. Many of the court equipages had already taken the road for Riga, whither the Empress intended to go. But on her return from Roguervick she suddenly changed her mind. Many people tormented their brains, in vain, to discover the cause of this change. Several years afterwards it came to light. When M. Tchoglokoff was passing through Riga, a Lutheran priest, a madman or a fanatic, placed in his hands a letter and a memorial addressed to the Empress, in which he exhorted her not to undertake this journey, as if she did she would incur the most imminent risk; that there were people posted in ambush by the enemies of the empire for the purpose of killing her, and such like absurdities. These writings, being delivered to the Empress, left her in no humour for travelling farther. As for the priest, he was found to be mad; but the journey did not take place.

We returned by short stages from Reval to St. Petersburg. I caught in this journey a severe sore throat, which compelled me to keep my bed for several days; after which we went to Peterhoff, and thence made weekly excursions to Oranienbaum.

At the beginning of August the Empress sent word to the Grand Duke and myself that we ought to go to our duty. We both complied with her wishes, and immediately began to have matins and vespers sung in our apartments, and to go to mass every day. On the Friday, when we were to go to confession, the cause of this order became apparent. Simon Theodorsky, Bishop of Pleskov, questioned us both a great deal, and each separately, respecting what had passed between the Czernicheffs and us. But as nothing whatever had passed, he looked a little foolish when he heard it asserted, with the candour of innocence, that there was not even the shadow of what people had dared to suppose. He was so far thrown off his guard as to say to me, "But how then is it that the Empress has been impressed to the contrary?" To which I replied, that I really did not know. I suppose our confessor communicated our confession to the Empress' confessor, and that the latter retailed it to her Majesty—a thing which certainly could do us no harm. We communicated on the Saturday, and on the Monday went for a week to Oranienbaum, while the Empress made an excursion to Zarskoe-Selo.

On arriving at Oranienbaum the Grand Duke enlisted all his suite. The chamberlains, the gentlemen of the bed-chamber, the officers of the court, the adjutants of Prince Repnine, and even his son, the servants, the huntsmen, the gardeners, every one, in fact, had to shoulder his musket. His Imperial Highness exercised them every day, and made them mount guard, the corridor of the house serving as a guard-room, and here they passed the day. For their meals the gentlemen went up stairs, and in the evening they came into the hall to dance in gaiters. As for ladies there were only myself, Madame Tchoglokoff, the Princess Repnine, my three maids of honour, and my lady's-maids; consequently the ball was very meagre and badly managed, the men harassed and in bad humour with these continual military exercises, which did not suit the taste of courtiers. After the ball they were allowed to go home to sleep. Generally speaking, we were all dreadfully tired of the dull life we led at Oranienbaum, where we were, five or six women, all to ourselves; while the men, on their side, were engaged in unwilling exercises. I had recourse to the books I had brought with me. Since my marriage I read a great deal. The first book I read after my marriage was a novel called Tiran the Fair (Tiran le blanc), and for a whole year I read nothing but novels. But I began to tire of these. I stumbled by accident upon the letters of Madame de Sévigné, and was much interested by them. When I had devoured these, the works of Voltaire fell into my hands. After reading them, I selected my books with more care.

We returned to Peterhoff, and after two or three journeys backwards and forwards, between that place and Oranienbaum, with the same amusements, we finally got back to St. Petersburg, and took up our residence in the Summer Palace.

At the close of autumn the Empress passed to the Winter Palace, where she occupied our apartments of the previous year; while we moved into those occupied by the Grand Duke before our marriage. These we liked very much, and, indeed, they were very convenient. They were those used by the Empress Anne. Every evening the members of our court assembled in our apartments, and we amused ourselves with all kinds of small games, or we had a concert. Twice a-week there was a performance at the great theatre, which at that time was opposite the church of Kasan. In a word, this winter was one of the gayest and best managed I have ever spent. We literally did nothing but laugh and romp the whole day.

About the middle of the winter, the Empress sent us word to follow her to Tichvine, where she was going. It was a journey of devotion; but just as we were about to enter our sledges, we learnt that the journey was put off. It was whispered to us that the Master of the Hounds, Count Razoumowsky, had got a fit of the gout, and that her Majesty did not wish to go without him. About two or three weeks afterwards we did start. The journey lasted only five days, when we returned. In passing through Ribatchia Slobodk, and by the house where I knew the Czernicheffs were, I tried to see them through the windows, but I could see nothing. Prince Repnine was not in the party during this journey; we were told that he had the gravel. The husband of Madame Tchoglokoff took his place on the occasion, and this was not the most agreeable arrangement in the world for most of us. He was an arrogant and brutal fool; everybody feared him, and his wife as well; and indeed, they were both mischievous and dangerous characters. However, there were means, as will be seen in the sequel, not only of lulling these Arguses to sleep, but even of gaining them over. At that time these means had not been discovered. One of the surest was to play at faro with them; they were both eager players, and very selfish ones. This weak point was the one first perceived; the others came afterwards.

During this winter, the Princess Gagarine, maid of honour, died of a burning fever, just as she was to be married to the Chamberlain Prince Galitzine, who subsequently married her younger sister. I regretted her very much, and during her illness I went several times to see her, notwithstanding the representations of Madame Tchoglokoff. The Empress replaced her by her elder sister, since married to count Matiuschkine. She was then at Moscow, and was sent for accordingly.

In the spring, we went to the Summer Palace, and thence to the country. Prince Repnine, under the pretext of bad health, received permission to retire to his own house, and M. Tchoglokoff continued to discharge his functions in the interim. He first signalized himself by the dismissal from our court of Count Divier, who was placed as brigadier in the army, and of the Gentleman of the Bedchamber Villebois, who was sent there as colonel. These changes were made at the instigation of Tchoglokoff, who looked on both with an evil eye, because he saw that we thought well of them. A similar dismissal had taken place in 1745, in the case of Count Zachar Czernicheff, sent away at the request of my mother. Still these removals were always considered at court as disgraces, and they were therefore sensibly felt by the individuals. The Grand Duke and myself were much annoyed with this latter one. Prince Augustus, too, having obtained all he had asked for, was told from the Empress that he must now leave. This also was a manœuvre of the Tchoglokoffs, who were bent upon completely isolating us. In this they followed the instructions of Count Bestoujeff, who was suspicious of everybody.

During this summer, having nothing better to do, and everything being very dull at home, I took a passion for riding; the rest of my time I spent in my room, reading everything that came in my way. As for the Grand Duke, as they had taken from him the people he liked best, he chose other favourites among the servants of the court.

During this interval, my valet Yevreinoff, while dressing my hair one day, told me that by a strange accident he had discovered that Andrew Czernicheff and his brothers were at Ribatchia, under arrest, in a pleasure-house, which was the private property of the Empress, who had inherited it from her mother. It was thus that the discovery was made:—During the carnival, Yevreinoff went out for a drive, having his wife and sister-in-law with him in the sledge, and the two brothers-in-law behind. The sister's husband was secretary to the Magistrate of St. Petersburg, and had a sister married to an under-secretary of the secret Chancery. They went for a walk one day to Ribatchia, and called on the man who had charge of this estate of the Empress. A dispute arose about the Feast of Easter, as to what day it would fall on. The host said that he would soon end the controversy by asking the prisoners for a book called Swiatzj, which contained all the Feasts, together with the calendar, for several years. In a few minutes he brought it in. The brother-in-law of Yevreinoff took the book, and the first thing he saw, on opening it, was that Andrew Czernicheff had put his name in it, with the date of the day on which he had received it from the Grand Duke. After this he looked for the Feast of Easter. The dispute being ended, the book was sent back, and they returned to St. Petersburg, where some days later, the brother-in-law of Yevreinoff confided to him the discovery he had made. Yevreinoff entreated me not to mention the matter to the Grand Duke, as his discretion was not at all to be relied on. I promised him that I would not, and kept my word.

About the middle of Lent, we went with the Empress to Gostilitza, to celebrate the feast-day of the Master of the Hounds, Count Razoumowsky. We danced, and were tolerably well amused, and then returned to town.

A few days afterwards, the death of my father was announced to me. It greatly afflicted me. For a week I was allowed to weep as much as I pleased, but at the end of that time, Madame Tchoglokoff came to tell me that I had wept enough; that the Empress ordered me to leave off; that my father was not a king. I told her I knew that he was not a king, and she replied that it was not suitable for a Grand Duchess to mourn for a longer period a father who had not been a king. In fine, it was arranged that I should go out on the following Sunday, and wear mourning for six weeks. The first day I left my room, I found Count Santi, Grand Master of Ceremonies to the Empress, in her Majesty's ante-chamber. I addressed a few casual remarks to him, and passed on. Some days later, Madame Tchoglokoff came to tell me that her Majesty had learned from Count Bestoujeff—to whom Santi had given the information in writing—that I had told him (Santi) I thought it very strange that the ambassadors had not offered their condolences to me on the occasion of my father's death; that her Majesty considered my remarks to Count Santi very uncalled for; that I was too proud; that I ought to remember that my father was not a king, and therefore that I could not and must not expect to receive the condolences of the foreign ministers. I was astounded at this speech. I told Madame Tchoglokoff that, if Count Santi had said or written that I had spoken to him a single word having the least allusion to this subject, he was a notorious liar; that nothing of the kind had entered my mind; and therefore that I had not uttered a syllable to him or any one else in reference to it. This was the exact truth, for I had laid it down to myself as an invariable rule never, in any case, to make any pretensions, but to conform in everything to the wishes of the Empress, and fulfil all her commands. It would seem that the ingenuousness with which I replied to Madame Tchoglokoff carried conviction to her mind, for she said she would not fail to tell the Empress that I gave the lie to Count Santi. In fact, she went to her Majesty, and came back to tell me that the Empress was extremely angry with Count Santi for having uttered such a falsehood, and that she had ordered him to be reprimanded. Some days afterwards, the Count sent several persons to me, and among them the Chamberlain, Count Nikita Panine, and the Vice-Chancellor, Woronzoff, to tell me that Count Bestoujeff had forced him to tell this falsehood, and that he was sorry to find himself in disgrace with me in consequence. I told these gentlemen that a liar was a liar, whatever might be his reasons for lying; and that, in order that Count Santi might not again mix me up with his falsehoods, I should never speak to him. Here is what has occurred to me in reference to this matter: Santi was an Italian. He was fond of intermeddling, and attached much importance to his office of Grand Master of Ceremonies. I had always spoken to him as I spoke to every one else. He thought, perhaps, that compliments of condolence on the part of the diplomatic corps might be admissible; and, judging by his own feelings, he probably considered that this would be a means of obliging me. He went then to Count Bestoujeff, the High Chancellor, and his superior, and told him that I had appeared in public for the first time, and seemed very much affected; the omission of the condolences might have added to my grief. Count Bestoujeff, always carping, and delighted to have an opportunity of humbling me, had all that Santi said or insinuated—and which he had ventured to support with my name—put into writing, and made him sign this protocol. Santi, terribly afraid of his superior, and above all things dreading to lose his place, did not hesitate to sign a falsehood rather than sacrifice his means of existence. The High Chancellor sent the note to the Empress. She was annoyed to see my pretensions, and despatched Madame Tchoglokoff to me, as already mentioned. But having heard my reply, founded upon the exact truth, the only result was a slap in the face for his excellency the Grand Master of the Ceremonies.

In the country, the Grand Duke formed a pack of hounds, and began to train dogs himself. When tired of tormenting these, he set to work scraping on the violin. He did not know a note, but he had a good ear, and made the beauty of music consist in the force and violence with which he drew forth the tones of his instrument. Those who had to listen to him, however, would often have been glad to stop their ears had they dared, for his music grated on them dreadfully. This course of life continued not only in the country, but also in town. On returning to the Winter Palace, Madame Krause—who had all along been an Argus—moderated so far as often even to aid in deceiving the Tchoglokoffs, who were hated by every one. She did more: she procured for the Grand Duke playthings—puppets, and such like childish toys, of which he was passionately fond. During the day, they were concealed within, or under my bed; the Grand Duke retired immediately after supper, and as soon as we were in bed Madame Krause locked the door, and then the Grand Duke played with his puppets till one or two o'clock in the morning. Willing or unwilling, I was obliged to share in this interesting amusement; and so was Madame Krause. I often laughed, but more frequently felt annoyed, and even inconvenienced; the whole bed was covered and filled with playthings, some of which were rather heavy. I do not know whether Madame Tchoglokoff came to hear of these nocturnal amusements, but one night, about twelve o'clock, she knocked at the door of our bed room. We did not open it immediately, as the Grand Duke, myself, and Madame Krause were scrambling with all our might to gather up and conceal the toys: for this purpose the cover-lid of the bed answered very well, as we crammed them all in under it. This done, we opened the door. She complained dreadfully of having been kept waiting, and told us that the Empress would be very angry when she learnt that we were not asleep at that hour. She then sulkily departed, without having made any further discovery. As soon as she was gone, the Duke resumed his amusements until he became sleepy.

At the commencement of autumn we again returned to the apartments which we had occupied after our marriage, in the Winter Palace. Here, a very stringent order was issued by the Empress through M. Tchoglokoff, forbidding every one from entering either my apartments or those of the Grand Duke, without the express permission of M. and Madame Tchoglokoff. The ladies and gentlemen of our court were directed, under pain of dismissal, to keep in the ante-chamber, and not to pass the threshold, or speak to us—or even to the servants—otherwise than aloud. The Grand Duke and myself, thus compelled to sit looking at each other, murmured, and secretly interchanged thoughts relative to this species of imprisonment, which neither of us had deserved. To procure for himself more amusement during the winter, the Duke had five or six hounds brought from the country, and placed them behind a wooden partition which separated the alcove of my bed-room from a large vestibule behind our apartments. As the alcove was separated only by boards, the odour of the kennel penetrated into it; and in the midst of this disgusting smell we both slept. When I complained to him of the inconvenience, he told me it was impossible to help it. The kennel being a great secret, I put up with this nuisance, rather than betray his Imperial Highness.

As there was no kind of amusement at court during this carnival, the Grand Duke took it into his head to have masquerades in my room. He dressed his servants, mine, and my maids in masks, and made them dance in my bed-room. He himself played the violin, and danced as well. All this continued far into the night. As for me, under different pretexts of headache or lassitude, I lay down on a couch, but always in a masquerade dress, tired to death of the insipidity of these *bal-masqués*, which amused him infinitely. When Lent came on, four more persons were removed from attendance on him, three of them being pages, whom he liked better than the others. These frequent dismissals affected him; still he took no steps to prevent them, or he took them so clumsily that they only tended to increase the evil.

During this winter, we learnt that Prince Repnine, ill as he was, had been appointed to command the troops which were to be sent to Bohemia, in aid of the Empress-Queen Maria Theresa. This was a formal disgrace for Prince Repnine. He went, and never returned, having died of grief in Bohemia. It was the Princess Gagarine, my maid of honour, who gave me the first intimation of this, notwithstanding all the prohibitions against allowing a word to reach us relative to what occurred in the city or the court. This shows how useless are all such prohibitions. There are too many persons interested in infringing them ever to allow of their being strictly enforced. All about us, even to the nearest relatives of the Tchoglokoffs, interested themselves in diminishing the rigour of the kind of political imprisonment to which we were subjected. There was no one, not even excepting Madame Tchoglokoff's own brother, Count Hendrikoff, who did not contrive to give us useful intimations; and many persons even made use of him to convey information to me, which he was always ready to do with the frankness of a good and honest fellow. He ridiculed the stupidities and brutalities of his sister and brother-in-law in such a manner that every one was at ease with him, and no one ever thought of distrusting him, for he never compromised any one, nor had any person ever been disappointed in him. He was a man of correct but limited judgment, ill-bred, and very ignorant, but firm, and without any evil.

During this same Lent, one day about noon, I went into the room where our ladies and gentlemen were assembled—the Tchoglokoffs had not yet come—and in speaking first to one and then to another, I approached the door near which the Chamberlain Outzine was standing. In a low voice he turned the conversation to the subject of the dull life we led, and said, that notwithstanding all this, people contrived to prejudice us in the mind of the Empress; that a few days before, her Imperial Majesty had said at table that I was overwhelmed with debt; that every thing I did bore the stamp of folly; that for all that I thought myself very clever—an opinion, however, in which no one else shared, for nobody was deceived in me, my stupidity being patent to all; and therefore that it was less necessary to mind what the Grand Duke did than what I did. He added, with tears in his eyes, that he was ordered by the Empress to tell me all this, but he begged me not to let it be supposed that he had told me of this order. I replied, that as to my stupidity it ought not to be objected to me as a fault, every one being just what God had made him; that as to my debts it was not very surprising I should be in debt when, with an allowance of 30,000 roubles, my mother, at parting, left me to pay 6,000 roubles on her account, while the Countess Roumianzoff had led me into innumerable expenses which she considered as indispensable; that Madame Tchoglokoff alone cost me this year 17,000 roubles, and that he himself knew what infernal play one was constantly obliged to play with them; that he might say all this to those who had sent him; that for the rest, I was very sorry I had been prejudiced in the opinion of her Imperial Majesty, to whom I had never failed in respect, obedience, and deference, and that the more closely my conduct was looked into the more would she be convinced of this. I promised him the secrecy he asked for, and kept it. I do not know whether he reported what I told him, but I fancy he did, though I heard no more of the matter, and did not care to renew a conversation so little agreeable.

During the last week of Lent, I took the measles. I could not make my appearance at Easter, but received the communion in my room, on the Saturday. During this illness, Madame Tchoglokoff, though far advanced in pregnancy, scarcely ever left me, and did all she could to amuse me. I had then a little Kalmuck girl, of whom I was very fond. She caught the measles from me. After Easter, we went to the Summer Palace, and thence, at the end of May—for the Feast of the Ascension—to the residence of the Count Razoumowsky, at Gostilitza. The Empress invited there, on the 23rd of this month, the Ambassador of the Imperial Court, the Baron Breitlack, who was about to leave for Vienna. He spent the evening there, and supped with the Empress. This supper was served at a very late hour, and we returned to the cottage in which we were lodged after sunrise. This cottage was of wood, placed on a slight elevation, and attached to the slides.

We had been pleased with the situation of this cottage when we were here in the winter, for the fête of the Master of the Hounds; and, in order to gratify us, he had placed us in it on the present occasion. It had two stories; the upper one consisted of a staircase, a saloon, and three cabinets. In one of these we slept, the Grand Duke used another as a dressing-room, and Madame Krause occupied the third. Below were lodged the Tchoglokoffs, my maids of honour, and my lady's-maids. On our return from supper, every one retired to rest. About six o'clock in the morning, a sergeant in the guards, Levacheff, arrived from Oranienbaum, to speak to Tchoglokoff relative to the buildings which were in the course of erection there. Finding every one asleep in the house, he sat down by the sentinel, and heard certain crackling noises, which excited his suspicions. The sentinel told him that these cracklings had been several times renewed since he had been on duty. Levacheff got up, and ran to the outside of the house. He saw that large blocks of stone were detaching themselves from the lower portion. He ran and woke Tchoglokoff, telling him that the foundations of the house were giving way, and that he must try and get every one out of it. Tchoglokoff put on a dressing-gown, and ran up stairs; where, finding the doors—which were of glass—locked, he burst them open. He thus reached our room, and drawing the curtains, desired us to get up as fast as possible and leave the house, as the foundations were giving way. The Grand Duke leaped out of bed, seized his dressing-gown, and ran off. I told Tchoglokoff that I would follow him, and he left me. While dressing I recollected that Madame Krause slept in the next room, and went to call her. She was so sound asleep that I had much difficulty in waking her, and then in making her understand that she must leave the house. I helped her to dress. When she was in a condition to go out, we passed into the drawing-room; but we had scarcely done so, when there was a universal crash, accompanied by a noise like that made by a vessel launched from the docks. We both fell on the ground. At the moment of our fall, Levacheff entered by the staircase door, which was opposite us. He raised me up, and carried me out of the room. I accidentally cast my eyes towards the slides: they had been on a level with the second story; they were so no longer but some two or three feet below it. Levacheff reached with me as far as the stairs by which he had ascended; they were no longer to be found, they had fallen; but several persons having climbed upon the wreck, Levacheff passed me to the nearest, these to the others, and thus from hand to hand I reached the bottom of the staircase in the hall, and thence was carried into a field. I there found the Grand Duke in his dressing-gown.

Once out of the house, I directed my attention to what was passing there, and saw several persons coming out of it all bloody, while others were carried out. Amongst those most severely wounded was the Princess Gagarine, my maid of honour. She had tried to escape like the rest, but in passing through a room adjoining her own, a stove, which fell down, overturned a screen, by which she was thrown upon a bed, which was in the room. Several bricks fell upon her head, and wounded her severely, as they did also a girl who was with her. In this same story there was a small kitchen, in which several servants slept, three of whom were killed by the fall of the fire-place. This, however, was nothing compared with what occurred between the foundations and the ground floor. Sixteen workmen attached to the slides slept there, and all of them were crushed to death by the fall of the house. All this mischief arose from the house having been built in the autumn, and in a hurry. They had given it as a foundation four layers of limestone. In the lower story the architect had placed, in the vestibule, twelve beams, which served as pillars. He had to go to the Ukraine, and at his departure told the manager of the estate of Gostilitza not to allow any one to touch those beams till his return. Yet, notwithstanding this prohibition, when the manager learnt we were to occupy this cottage, nothing would do but he must immediately remove these beams, because they disfigured the vestibule. Then, when the thaw came, everything sank upon the four layers of limestone, which gave way in different directions, and the entire building slid towards a hillock, which arrested its progress. I escaped with a few slight bruises and a great fright, for which I was bled. This fright was so general and so great amongst us all, that for more than four months afterwards, if a door was only slammed with a little extra force, every one started. On the day of the accident, when the first terror had passed, the Empress, who occupied another house, sent for us, and, as she wished to make light of the danger we had been in, every one tried to see little in it, and some none at all. My terror displeased her very much, and she was out of humour with me. The Master of the Hounds wept, and was inconsolable; he talked of blowing out his brains. I presume he was prevented, for he did nothing of the kind, and the next day we returned to St. Petersburg, and some weeks later to the Summer Palace.

I do not exactly remember, but I fancy it was about this time that the Chevalier Sacromoso arrived in Russia. It was a long time since a Knight of Malta had visited this country, and, generally speaking, few persons came to St. Petersburg in those days; his arrival, therefore, was a sort of event. He was received with marked attention, and was shown everything worthy of note in St. Petersburg and Cronstadt. A naval officer of distinction was appointed to accompany him. This was M. Poliansky, then captain of a man-of-war, since an admiral. He was presented to us. In kissing my hand he slipped into it a very small note, saying at the same time, in a low voice, "It is from your mother." I was almost stupefied with terror at this act. I dreaded its being observed by some one or other, especially by the Tchoglokoffs, who were close by. However, I took the note, and slipped it into my right hand glove; no one had noticed it. On returning to my room, I found, in fact, a letter from my mother, rolled up in a slip of paper, on which it was stated that the Chevalier expected an answer through an Italian musician, who attended the Grand Duke's concerts. My mother, rendered anxious by my involuntary silence, wanted to know the cause of it; she also wished to know in what situation I was. I wrote to her, giving her the information she required. I told her that I had been forbidden to write to any one, under the pretext that it did not become a Grand Duchess of Russia to write any letters but such as were composed at the Office of Foreign Affairs, where I was only to attach my signature, and never to dictate what was to be written, because the ministers knew better than I did what was proper to be said; that it had almost been made a crime in M. Olzoufieff that I had sent him a few lines, which I begged him to enclose in a letter to my mother. I also gave her information on several other points, about which she had inquired. I rolled up my note in the same manner as the one I had received, and watched with impatience and anxiety the moment for getting rid of it. At the first concert given by the Grand Duke, I made the tour of the orchestra, and stopped behind the chair of the solo violinist, D'Ologlio, who was the person pointed out to me. When he saw me come behind his chair, he pretended to take his handkerchief from his coat-pocket, and in doing so left his pocket wide open. Without any appearance of action, I slipped my note into it, and no one had the slightest suspicion of what had happened. During his stay in St. Petersburg, Sacromoso delivered to me two or three other notes having reference to the same matter;

my answers were returned in the same manner, and no one was ever the wiser.

From the Summer Palace we went to Peterhoff, which was then being rebuilt. We were lodged in the upper palace, in Peter the First's old house, which was standing at that time. Here, to pass the time, the Grand Duke took it into his head to play with me every afternoon at two-handed ombre. When I won he got angry, and when I lost he wanted to be paid forthwith. I had no money, so he began to play at games of hazard with me, quite by ourselves. I remember on one occasion his night-cap stood with us for 10,000 roubles; but when at the end of the game he was a loser, he became furious, and would sometimes sulk for many days. This kind of play was not in any way to my taste.

During this stay at Peterhoff we saw from our windows, which looked out upon the garden towards the sea, that M. and Madame Tchoglokoff were continually passing and repassing from the upper palace towards that of Monplaisir on the sea-shore, where the Empress was then residing. This excited our curiosity, and that of Madame Krause also, to know the object of all these journeys. For this purpose Madame Krause went to her sister's, who was head lady's-maid to the Empress. She returned quite radiant with pleasure, having learned that all these movements were occasioned by its having come to the knowledge of the Empress that M. Tchoglokoff had had an intrigue with one of my maids of honour, Mademoiselle Kocheleff, who was with child in consequence. The Empress had sent for Madame Tchoglokoff and told her that her husband deceived her, while she loved him like a fool; that she had been blind to such a degree as to have this girl, the favourite of her husband, almost living with her; that if she wished to separate from her husband at once it would not be displeasing to her Majesty, who even from the beginning had not regarded her marriage with M. Tchoglokoff with a favourable eye. Her Majesty declared to her point-blank that she did not choose him to continue with us, but would dismiss him and leave her in charge. Madame Tchoglokoff at first denied the passion of her husband, and maintained that the charge against him was a calumny; but in the meantime her Majesty had sent some one to question the young lady, who at once acknowledged the fact. This rendered Madame Tchoglokoff furious against her husband. She returned home and abused him. He fell upon his knees and begged her pardon, and made use of all his influence over her to soothe her anger. The brood of children which they had also helped to patch up their difference; but their reconciliation was never sincere. Disunited in love, they remained connected by interest. The wife pardoned her husband; she went to the Empress, and told her that she had forgiven everything, and wished to remain with him for the sake of her children. She entreated her Majesty on her knees not to dismiss him ignominiously from court, saying that this would be to disgrace her and complete her misery. In a word, she behaved so well on this occasion, and with such firmness and generosity, and her grief besides was so real, that she disarmed the anger of the Empress. She did more; she led her husband before her Imperial Majesty, told him many home truths, and then threw herself with him at the feet of her Majesty, and entreated her to pardon him for her sake and that of her six children, whose father he was. These different scenes lasted five or six days; and we learned, almost hour by hour, what was going on, because we were less watched during the time, as every one hoped to see these people dismissed. But the issue did not answer their expectations; no one was dismissed but the young lady, who was sent back to her uncle, the Grand Marshal of the Court, Chepeleff; while the Tchoglokoffs remained, less glorious, however, than they had been. The day of our departure for Oranienbaum was chosen for the dismissal of Mademoiselle Kocheleff; and while we set off in one direction, she went in another.

At Oranienbaum, we resided, this year, in the town, to the right and left of the main building, which was small. The affair of Gostilitza had given such a thorough fright, that orders had been issued to examine the floors and ceilings in all the houses belonging to the court, and to repair those which required attention.

This is the kind of life I led at Oranienbaum: I rose at three o'clock in the morning, and dressed myself alone from head to foot in male attire; an old huntsman whom I had was already waiting for me with the guns; a fisherman's skiff was ready on the sea-shore: we traversed the garden on foot, with our guns upon our shoulders; entered the boat together with a fisherman and a pointer, and I shot ducks in the reeds which bordered on both sides the canal of Oranienbaum, which extends two verstes into the sea. We often doubled this canal, and consequently were occasionally, for a considerable time, in the open sea in this skiff. The Grand Duke came an hour or two after us; for he must needs always have a breakfast and God knows what besides, which he dragged after him. If we met we went together, if not each shot and hunted alone. At ten o'clock, and often later, I returned and dressed for dinner. After dinner we rested; and in the evening the Grand Duke had music, or we rode out on horseback. Having led this sort of life for about a week, I felt myself very much heated and my head confused. I saw that I required repose and dieting; so for four-and-twenty hours I ate nothing, drank only cold water, and for two nights slept as long as I could.

After this I recommenced the same course of life, and found myself quite well. I remember reading at that time the Memoirs of Brantôme, which greatly amused me. Before that I had read the Life of Henri IV. by Périfix.

Towards autumn we returned to town, and learned that we were to go to Moscow in the course of the winter. Madame Krause came to tell me that it was necessary to increase my stock of linen for this journey. I entered into the details of the matter; Madame Krause pretended to amuse me by having the linen cut up in my room, in order, as she said, to teach me how many chemises might be cut from a single piece of cloth. This instruction or amusement seems to have displeased Madame Tchoglokoff, who had become very ill-tempered since the discovery of her husband's infidelity. I know not what she told the Empress; but, at all events, she came to me one afternoon and said that her Majesty had dispensed with Madame Krause's attendance on me, and that she was going to retire to the residence of her son-in-law the Chamberlain Sievers; and next day Madame Tchoglokoff brought Madame Vladislava to me to occupy her place. Madame Vladislava was a tall woman, apparently well formed, and with an intelligent cast of features, which rather prepossessed me at the first look. I consulted my oracle Timothy Yevreinoff relative to this choice. He told me that this woman, whom I had never before seen, was the mother-in-law of the Counsellor Pougovichnikoff, head clerk to Count Bestoujeff; that she was not wanting either in intelligence or sprightliness, but was considered very artful; that I must wait and see how she conducted herself, and especially be careful not to place much confidence in her. She was called Praskovia Nikitichna. She began very well; she was sociable, fond of talking, conversed and narrated with spirit, and had at her fingers' ends, all the anecdotes of the time, past and present. She knew four or five generations of all the families, could give at a moment everybody's genealogy, father, mother, grandfathers, grandmothers, together with their ancestors, paternal and maternal; and from no one else have I received so much information relative to all that has occurred in Russia for the last hundred years. The mind and manners of this woman suited me very well; and when I felt dull I made her chat, which she was always ready to do. I easily discovered that she very often disapproved of the sayings and doings of the Tchoglokoffs; but as she also went very often to her Majesty's apartments, no one knew why, we were obliged to be on our guard with her, to a certain degree, not knowing what interpretation might be put upon the most innocent words and actions.

From the Summer Palace we passed to the Winter Palace. Here was presented to us Madame La Tour l'Annois, who had been in attendance on the Empress in her early youth, and had accompanied the Princess Anna Petrovna, eldest daughter of Peter I., when she left Russia with her husband, the Duke of Holstein, during the reign of the Emperor Peter II. After the death of this Princess, Madame l'Annois returned to France, and she now came to Russia, either to remain there, or possibly to return after having obtained some favours from her Majesty. Madame l'Annois hoped, on the ground of old acquaintance, to re-enter into the favour and familiarity of the Empress. But she was greatly deceived; every one conspired to exclude her. From the first few days after her arrival I foresaw what would happen, and for this reason: One evening, while they were at cards in the Empress' apartment, her Majesty continued moving from room to room without fixing herself anywhere, as was her custom; Madame l'Annois, hoping, no doubt, to pay her court to her, followed her wherever she went. Madame Tchoglokoff seeing this, said to me, "See how that woman follows the Empress everywhere; but that will not continue long, she will very soon drop that habit of running after her." I took this as settled, and, in fact, she was first kept at a distance, and finally sent back to France with presents. During this winter was celebrated the marriage of Count Lestocq with Mademoiselle Mengden, Maid of Honour to the Empress. Her Majesty and the whole court assisted at it, and she paid the newly-married couple the honour of visiting them at their own house. One would have said that they enjoyed the highest favour, but in a couple of months afterwards fortune turned. One evening, while looking on at those engaged at play in the apartments of the Empress, I saw the Count, and advanced to speak to him. "Do not come near me," he said in a low tone, "I am a suspected man." I thought he must be jesting, and asked what he meant. He replied, "I tell you quite seriously not to come near me, because I am a suspected man, whom people must shun." I saw that he had an altered look, and was extremely red. I fancied he must have been drinking, and turned away. This happened on the Friday. On the Sunday morning, while dressing my hair, Timothy Yevreinoff said to me, "Are you aware that last night Count Lestocq and his wife were arrested, and conducted to the Fortress as state criminals?" No one knew why, but it became known that General Stephen Apraxine and Alexander Schouvaloff had been named commissioners for this affair.

The departure of the court for Moscow was fixed for the 16th of December. The Czernicheffs had been transported to the Fortress, and placed in a house belonging to the Empress, called Smolnoy Dvoretz. The elder of the three sometimes made his guards drunk, and then went and walked into town to his friends. One day, a Finnish wardrobe-maid, who was in my service, and was engaged to be married to a servant belonging to the court, a relation of Yevreinoff, brought me a letter from Andrew Czernicheff, in which he asked me for several things. This girl had seen him at the house of her intended, where they had spent the evening together. I was at a loss where to conceal this letter when I got it, for I did not like to burn it, as I wanted to remember what he asked for. I had long been forbidden to write even to my mother. I purchased, through this girl, a silver pen and an inkstand. During the day I had the letter in my pocket; when I undressed, I slipped it under my garter, into my stocking, and before going to bed I removed it, and placed it in my sleeve. At last I answered it; sent him what he asked for through the channel by which his letter had reached me, and then, at a favourable moment, burned this letter which had occasioned me so much anxiety.

About the middle of December we set out for Moscow. The Grand Duke and I occupied a large sledge, and the gentlemen in waiting sat in the front. During the day the Grand Duke joined M. Tchoglokoff in a town sledge, while I remained in the large one. As we never closed this, I conversed with those who were seated in front. I remember that the Chamberlain, Prince Alexander Jourievitch Troubetzkoy, told me, during this time, that Count Lestocq, then a prisoner in the Fortress, wanted to starve himself during the first eleven days of his detention, but that he had been forced to take nourishment: he had been accused of having accepted 1,000 roubles from the King of Prussia to support his interests, and for having had a person named Oettinger, who might have borne witness against him, poisoned. He was subjected to the torture, and then exiled to Siberia.

In this journey, the Empress passed us at Tver, and as the horses and provisions intended for us were taken by her suite, we remained twenty-four hours at Tver without horses, and without food. We were dreadfully hungry. Towards night Tchoglokoff had prepared for us a roasted sturgeon, which we thought delicious. We set off at night, and reached Moscow two or three days before Christmas. The first thing we heard there was, that the Chamberlain of our Court, Prince Alex. Mich. Galitzine, had received, at the moment of our departure from St. Petersburg, an order to repair to Hamburg as minister of Russia, with a salary of 4,000 roubles. This was looked upon as another case of banishment: his sister-in-law, Princess Gagarine, who was with me, grieved very much, and we all regretted him.

We occupied at Moscow the apartments which I had inhabited with my mother in 1744. To go to the great church of the court, it was necessary to make the circuit of the house in a carriage. On Christmas-day, at the hour for mass, we were on the point of descending to our carriage, and were already on the stairs, during a frost of 29 degrees, when a message came from the Empress to say that she dispensed with our going to church on this occasion, on account of the extreme cold; it did, in fact, pinch our noses. I was obliged to keep my room during the early portion of our residence in Moscow, on account of the excessive quantity of pimples which had come on my face: I was dreadfully afraid of having to continue with a pimpled face. I called in the physician Boërhave, who gave me sedatives, and all sorts of things to dispel these pimples. At last, when nothing was of avail, he said to me one day, "I am going to give you something which will drive them away." He drew from his pocket a small phial of oil of Falk, and told me to put a drop in a cup of water, and to wash my face with it from time to time, say, for instance, once a-week. And really the oil of Falk did clear my face, and by the end of some ten days I was able to appear. A short time after our arrival in Moscow (1749), Madam Vladislava came to tell me that the Empress had ordered the marriage of my Finnish wardrobe-maid to take place as soon as possible. The only apparent reason for thus hastening her marriage was, that I had shown some predilection for her; for she was a merry creature, who from time to time made me laugh by mimicking every one, Madame Tchoglokoff especially being hit off in a very amusing manner. She was married, then, and no more said about her.

In the middle of the Carnival, during which there were no amusements whatever, the Empress was seized with a violent cholic, which threatened to be serious. Madame Vladislava and Timothy Yevreinoff each whispered this in my ear, entreating me not to mention to any one who had told me. Without naming them, I informed the Grand Duke of it, and he became very much elated. One morning, Yevreinoff came to tell me that the Chancellor Bestoujeff and General Apraxine had passed the previous night in the apartment of M. and Madame Tchoglokoff, which seemed to imply that the Empress was very ill. Tchoglokoff and his wife were more gruff than ever; they came into our apartments, dined there, supped, but never allowed a word to escape them relative to this illness. We did not speak of it either, and consequently did not dare to send and inquire how her Majesty was, because we should have been immediately asked, "How, whence, by whom came you to learn, that she was ill?" and any one named, or even suspected, would infallibly have been dismissed, exiled, or even sent to the Secret Chancery, that state inquisition, more dreaded than death itself. At last her Majesty, at the end of ten days, became better, and the wedding of one of her maids of honour took place at court. At table I was seated by the side of the Countess Schouvaloff, the favourite of the Empress. She told me that her Majesty was still so weak from the severe illness she had just had, that she had placed her diamonds on the bride's head (an honour which she paid to all her maids of honour) while seated in bed, her feet only being outside; and that it was for this reason she was not present at the wedding-feast. As the Countess Schouvaloff was the first to speak to me of this illness, I expressed to her the pain which her Majesty's condition gave me, and the interest I took in it. She said her Majesty would be pleased to learn how much I felt for her. Two mornings after this, Madame Tchoglokoff came to my room, and, in the presence of Madame Vladislava, told me that the Empress was very angry with the Grand Duke and myself on account of the little interest we had taken in her illness, even carrying our indifference to such an extent as not once to send and inquire how she was. I told Madame Tchoglokoff that I appealed to herself, that neither she nor her husband had spoken a single word to us about the illness of her Majesty, and that knowing nothing of it, we had not been able to testify our interest in it. She replied, "How can you say that you knew nothing of it, when the Countess Schouvaloff has informed her Majesty that you spoke to her at table about it." I replied, "It is true that I did so, because she told me her Majesty was still weak and could not leave her room, and then I asked her the particulars of this illness." Madame Tchoglokoff went away grumbling, and Madame Vladislava said it was very strange to try and pick a quarrel with people about a matter of which they were ignorant; that since the Tchoglokoffs alone had the right to speak of it, and did not speak, the fault was theirs, not ours, if we failed through ignorance. Some time afterwards, on a court-day, the Empress approached me, and I found a favourable moment for telling her that neither Tchoglokoff nor his wife had given us any intimation of her illness, and that therefore it had not been in our power to express to her the interest we had taken in it. She received this very well, and it seemed to me that the credit of these people was diminishing.

The first week of Lent, M. Tchoglokoff wished to go to his duty. He confessed, but the confessor of the Empress forbade him to communicate. The whole court said it was by the order of her Majesty, on account of his adventure with Mademoiselle Kocheleff. During a portion of our stay at Moscow, M. Tchoglokoff appeared to be intimately connected with Count Bestoujeff and his tool General Stephen Apraxine. He was continually with them, and, to hear him speak, one would have supposed him to be the intimate adviser of Count Bestoujeff—a thing that was quite impossible, for Bestoujeff had far too much sense to allow himself to be guided by such an arrogant fool as Tchoglokoff. But, at about half the period of our stay, this intimacy suddenly ceased—I do not exactly know why— and Tchoglokoff became the sworn enemy of those with whom he had been so intimate a short time previously.

Shortly after my arrival in Moscow, I began, for want of other amusement, to read the History of Germany, by le Père Barre, canon of Ste. Geneviève, in nine volumes quarto. Every week I finished one, after which I read the works of Plato. My rooms faced the street; the corresponding ones were occupied by the Duke, whose windows opened upon a small yard. When reading in my room, one of my maids usually came in, and remained there standing as long as she wished; she then retired, and another took her place when she thought it suitable. I made Madame Vladislava see that this routine could serve no useful purpose, but was merely an inconvenience; that, besides, I already had much to suffer from the proximity of my apartments to those of the Grand Duke, by which she, too, was equally discommoded, as she occupied a small cabinet at the end of my rooms. She consented, therefore, to relieve my maids from this species of etiquette. This is the kind of annoyance we had to put up with, morning, noon and night, even to a late hour: The Grand Duke, with rare perseverance, trained a pack of dogs, and with heavy blows of his whip, and cries like those of the huntsmen, made them fly from one end to the other of his two rooms, which were all he had. Such of the dogs as became tired, or got out of rank, were severely punished, which made them howl still more. When he got tired of this detestable exercise, so painful to the ears and destructive to the repose of his neighbours, he seized his violin, on which he rasped away with extraordinary violence, and very badly, all the time walking up and down his rooms. Then he recommenced the education and punishment of his dogs, which to me seemed very cruel. On one occasion, hearing one of these animals howl piteously and for a long time, I opened the door of my bed-room, where I was seated, and which adjoined the apartment in which this scene was enacted, and saw him holding this dog by the collar, suspended in the air, while a boy who was in his service, a Kalmuck by birth, held the animal by the tail. It was a poor little King Charles's dog of English breed, and the Duke was beating him with all his might with the heavy handle of a whip. I interceded for the poor beast, but this only made him redouble his blows. Unable to bear so cruel a scene, I returned to my room with tears in my eyes. In general, tears and cries, instead of moving the Duke to pity, put him in a passion. Pity was a feeling that was painful, and even insupportable in his mind.

About this time, my valet Timothy Yevreinoff transmitted to me a letter from his old comrade Andrew Czernicheff, who had at last been set at liberty, and was passing near Moscow, to join the regiment in which he had been placed as lieutenant. I managed with this letter as with the former one, sent him all he asked for, and never mentioned a word about the matter either to the Grand Duke or any one else.

In the spring, the Empress took us to Perova, where we spent some days with her at the residence of Count Razoumowsky. The Grand Duke and M. Tchoglokoff scoured the woods almost daily, accompanied by the master of the house. I read in my room, or else Madame Tchoglokoff, when she was not at cards, came and kept me company to dissipate her ennui. She complained bitterly of the amusements of this place, and especially of the constant indulgence of her husband in the sports of the chase, for he had become a passionate sportsman since he had received at Moscow the present of a beautiful English greyhound. I learned from others that he was the laughing-stock of all the sportsmen, and that he fancied, and was made to believe that his Circe (the name of his dog) caught all the hares that were taken. In general, M. Tchoglokoff was very apt to believe that everything belonging to him was of rare beauty and excellence; his wife, his children, his servants, his house, his table, his horses, his dogs—everything that was his, although in reality very mediocre, participated in his self love, and, as belonging to him, became in his eyes of incomparable value.

One day, while at Perova, I was seized with a headache so violent that I do not remember ever having had anything like it in my life. The excessive pain brought on violent sickness. I threw up repeatedly, and every movement in my room made me worse. I remained in this state for nearly four-and-twenty hours, and then fell asleep. The next day I felt nothing but weakness. Madame Tchoglokoff took all possible care of me during this severe attack. Generally speaking, all the persons who had been placed about me by an ill-will the most unequivocal, began in a short time to take an involuntary interest in me; and, when they were not interfered with or stimulated anew, they used to act against the principles of their employers, and yield to the impulse which attracted them towards me, or rather to the interest with which I inspired them. They never found me sulky or peevish, but always ready to meet the slightest advance on their part. In all this my natural gaiety was of great service to me, for all these Arguses were often amused with my conversation, and relaxed in spite of themselves.

Her Majesty had a new attack of cholic at Perova. She was carried to Moscow, and we went slowly to the palace, which is only four verstes from there. This attack had no ill consequence, and shortly afterwards she made a pilgrimage to the convent of Troïtza. She wished to make these sixty verstes on foot, and for this purpose went to Pokrovskoe House. We were ordered to take the Troïtza road, and we took up our quarters on this road about eleven verstes from Moscow, at a very small country-house called Rajova, belonging to Madame Tchoglokoff. The only accommodations were a small saloon in the centre of the house, and two very small rooms on each side of it. Tents were placed round the house for the use of our suite. The Grand Duke had one; I occupied one of the little rooms, Madame Vladislava another, the Tchoglokoffs the remainder. We dined in the saloon. The Empress walked three or four verstes, then rested some days. This journey lasted nearly the whole summer. We hunted every day after dinner. When her Majesty reached Taïninskoe, which is nearly opposite Rajova, on the other side of the high road leading to the convent of Troïtza, the Hetman, Count Razoumowsky, younger brother of the favourite—who was residing at his country seat of Pokrovskoe, on the road to St. Petersburg, on the other side of Moscow—took it into his head to come and see us every day at Rajova. He was very gay, and nearly of our own age. We liked him very much. As brother of the favourite, M. and Madame Tchoglokoff willingly received him into their house. His assiduity continued all the summer, and we were always pleased to see him. He dined and supped with us, and after supper returned again to his estate; he consequently travelled forty or fifty verstes a-day. Some twenty years later, it occurred to me to ask him what it was that could then induce him to come and share the dulness and insipidity of our life at Rajova, while his own house was daily crowded with the best company at Moscow. He replied, unhesitatingly, "Love." "But what on earth could you have found to love at our house?" "What!" he said, "why, you." I burst into a loud laugh, for the idea had never once crossed my mind; besides he had been married for some years to a rich heiress of the house of Narichkine, whom the Empress had made him marry, a little against his will it is true, but with whom he seemed to live on good terms. Added to this, it was well known that the handsomest women of the court and city contended for his notice; and, indeed, he was a fine man, of an original turn, very agreeable, and with far more intelligence than his brother, who however equalled him in beauty, while surpassing him in generosity and kindness. These two brothers were the most generally liked favourites I have ever known.

About the Feast of St. Peter, the Empress sent us word to join her at Bratovchina. We repaired thither immediately.

As during the spring and a part of the summer I had either been engaged in sporting, or otherwise constantly in the open air, Rajova House being so small that we spent the greater part of the day in the neighbouring woods, I arrived at Bratovchina with my face very red and tanned. When the Empress saw me, she exclaimed against this redness, and said she would send me a wash to remove it, and she did so; she immediately sent a phial containing a liquid composed of lemon-juice, white of egg, and French brandy, and ordered that my maids should learn its composition, and the proper proportions of its ingredients. At the end of a few days my sun-burns had disappeared, and I have since used this composition, and recommended it to others for similar purposes. When the skin is heated, I do not know of a better remedy. It is also good for what they call in Russia Tetters, and which is nothing but a heating of the skin, which causes it to crack. I cannot at the moment recall the French term for this complaint.

We spent the Feast of St. Peter at the convent of Troïtza, and as the Grand Duke could find nothing to do after dinner, he took it into his head to have a ball in his own room, where, however, his only company were his two valets and my two maids, one of whom was over fifty. From the convent her Majesty went to Taïninskoe, while we returned to Rajova, and resumed our former mode of life. We remained there till the middle of August, when the Empress made a journey to Sophino, a place situated at sixty or seventy verstes from Moscow. Here we encamped. On the morning after our arrival we went to her Majesty's tent, and found her scolding the person who had the management of this estate. She had come here to hunt, and found no hares. The man was pale and trembling, and there was nothing that she did not say to him; she was really furious. Seeing that we had come to kiss her hand, she embraced us as usual, and then went on with her scolding, bringing within the sphere of her remarks every one she felt disposed to find fault with. This was done gradually, and while speaking with extreme volubility. She said, among other things, that she perfectly understood the management of land; that the reign of the Empress Anne had taught her this; that having but little, she took care to avoid extravagance; that had she gone in debt, she would have been afraid of being damned: for if she had died in such a condition no one would have paid her debts, and then her soul would have gone to hell, and that she had no fancy for; that therefore, when she was in the house, or not otherwise obliged to make an appearance, she dressed very simply, her outside dress being of white taffeta and the under of dark gray, and in this manner she economized, taking good care not to wear expensive clothes in the country or when travelling. This, of course, had reference to me, for I wore a dress of silvered lilac. I took the hint. This dissertation—for such it was, no one venturing to speak, seeing her flushed with passion—lasted more than three-quarters of an hour. At last, a fool she had, named Aksakoff, put a stop to it. He came in carrying a little porcupine, which he presented to her, in his hat. She advanced to look at it, but the instant she saw it she uttered a piercing cry, saying that it looked like a mouse, and ran precipitately into the interior of the tent, for she had a mortal antipathy to mice. We saw no more of her: she dined alone. After dinner she went to the chase, took the Grand Duke with her, and ordered me to return with Madame Tchoglokoff to Moscow, where the Grand Duke arrived some hours afterwards, the chase having been but brief, in consequence of the high wind that prevailed that day.

One Sunday the Empress sent for us to join her at Taïninskoe—we were then at Rajova, whither we had returned—and we had the honour of dining with her Majesty. She sat alone at the head of the table, the Grand Duke at her right, I at her left, opposite to him. Near the Grand Duke was Marshal Boutourline, near me the Countess Schouvaloff. The table was very long and narrow. Thus seated between the Empress and the Marshal, the Grand Duke, not a little aided by the Marshal, who was by no means an enemy to wine himself, managed to get exceedingly intoxicated. He neither knew what he said or did, stuttered in his speech, and made himself so very disagreeable, that tears came into my eyes; for at that time I concealed and palliated as much as possible all that was reprehensible in him. The Empress was pleased with my sensibility, and left the table earlier than usual. His Imperial Highness was to have gone hunting in the afternoon with Count Razoumowsky, but he remained at Taïninskoe, while I returned to Rajova. On the way I was seized with a violent toothache. The weather began to be cold and wet, and we were but badly sheltered at Rajova. The brother of Madame Tchoglokoff, Count Hendrikoff, who was the chamberlain on duty with me, proposed to his sister to cure me instantly. She spoke to me on the subject, and I consented to try his remedy, which seemed to be nothing at all, or rather a mere charlatanism. He went immediately into the other room, and brought out a very small roll of paper, which he desired me to chew with the aching tooth. Hardly had I done so when the pain became so extremely violent that I was obliged to go to bed. I got into such a burning fever, that I began to be delirious. Madame Tchoglokoff, terrified at my condition, and attributing it to her brother's remedy, got very angry and abused him. She remained at my bedside all the night, sent word to the Empress that her house at Rajova was in no way fit for a person so seriously ill as I appeared to be, and in fact made such a stir, that the next day I was removed to Moscow very ill. I was ten or twelve days in bed, and the toothache returned every afternoon at the same hour. At the beginning of September, the Empress went to the convent of Voskressensky, whither we were ordered to go for the feast of her name. On that day M. Iran Ivanovitch Schouvaloff was declared a Gentleman of the Bedchamber. This was an event at court. Every one whispered that a new favourite had appeared. I was rejoiced at his promotion, for, while he was a page, I had marked him out as a person of promise, on account of his studiousness; he was always to be seen with a book in his hand.

Having returned from this excursion, I was seized with a sore throat accompanied with much fever. The Empress came to see me during this illness. When barely convalescent, and while still very weak, her Majesty ordered me, through Madame Tchoglokoff, to assist at the wedding and dress the hair of the niece of the Countess Roumianzoff, who was about to be married to M. Alexander Narichkine, subsequently created chief cupbearer. Madame Tchoglokoff, who saw that I was scarcely convalescent, was a little pained in announcing to me this compliment, a compliment which gave me but little pleasure, as it plainly showed how little was cared for my health, perhaps even for my life. I spoke in this view to Madame Vladislava, who seemed, like myself, but little pleased with this order, an order evidently given without care or consideration. I exerted myself, however, and on the day fixed the bride was led to my room. I adorned her head with my diamonds, and she was then conducted to the court church to be married. As for me, I had to go to Narichkine House, accompanied by Madame Tchoglokoff and my own court. Now, we were living at Moscow, in the palace at the end of the German Sloboda. To reach the residence of the Narichkines it was necessary to go right through Moscow, and travel at least seven verstes. It was in the month of October, about nine o'clock at night. It froze excessively hard, and the ground was so slippery that we had to travel very slowly. We were at least two hours and a-half in going, and the same in returning, and there was not a man or horse in my suite that had not one or more falls. At last having reached the church of Kasansky, which was near the gate called Troïtzkaja, we met with another impediment, for in this church was married, at the very same hour, the sister of Ivan Ivanovitch Schouvaloff. Her hair had been dressed by the Empress herself, while I dressed that of Mademoiselle Roumianzoff. A great crowding of carriages occurred at this gate. We had to stop at every step; then the falls recommenced; not one of the horses had been rough shod. At last we reached the house, and not in the best humour in the world. We waited a long time for the bride and bridegroom, who had met with the same impediments as ourselves. The Grand Duke accompanied the bride. Then we waited for the Empress. At last we sat down to supper. After supper, there were a few rounds of dancing in the ante-chamber as a matter of ceremony, and then we were told to lead the bride and bridegroom to their apartments. For this purpose we had to pass along several cold corridors, mount staircases equally cold, and then traverse long galleries hastily constructed of damp boards, from which the water oozed in all directions. At last, having reached the apartments, we sat down to a table spread with a dessert, remaining only long enough to drink the health of the newly married. Then the bride was led to her chamber, and we returned home. The next evening we had to repeat our visit. Would any one have believed it? This turmoil, instead of injuring my health, did not in the least retard my convalescence. The following day I was better than the previous one.

At the beginning of winter, I saw that the Grand Duke was very much disturbed. I did not know what was the matter. He no longer trained his dogs. He came into my room twenty times a-day, looked anxious, thoughtful, and absent. He bought German books, and such books! One portion consisted of Lutheran prayer-books, the other of the history and trial of some highway robbers who had been hung or broken on the wheel. These he read by turns when not playing the violin. As he could not long keep on his mind anything which tormented him, and as he had no one to speak to but me, I waited patiently for his revelation.

At last he told me what it was that disturbed him, and I found the matter far more serious than I had anticipated. During the whole summer pretty nearly, at all events during our stay at Rajova, on the road to the convent of Troïtza, I scarcely ever saw him, except at table or in bed. He came to bed after I was asleep, and rose before I was awake. The rest of his time was passed in hunting or in preparations for it. Tchoglokoff had obtained, under pretext of amusing the Grand Duke, two packs of dogs from the Master of the Hounds, the one of Russian dogs and huntsmen, the other of French or German dogs. To the latter were attached an old French whipper-in, a lad from Courland, and a German. As M. Tchoglokoff took the direction of the Russian pack, the Grand Duke undertook that of the foreign one, about which Tchoglokoff did not in the least trouble himself. Each entered into the minutest details of his own charge, and the Grand Duke therefore was constantly going to the kennel of his pack, or the huntsmen were coming to him to inform him of its condition, and of the wants and deeds of the dogs. In a word, if I must speak plainly, he made himself the companion of these men, drinking with them in the chase, and being constantly among them.

The regiment of Boutirsky was then at Moscow. In this regiment was a lieutenant named Yakoff Batourine, a man overwhelmed with debt, a gambler, and well known to be a worthless fellow, but a very determined one. I know not how this man happened to get acquainted with the Grand Duke's huntsmen, but I believe both had their quarters in or near the village of Moutistcha or Alexeewsky. At last matters went on so far, that the huntsmen told the Duke there was a lieutenant in the regiment of Boutirsky who manifested a great attachment to his Imperial Highness, and who said, besides, that the entire regiment entertained the same feelings as himself. The Grand Duke listened to this recital with complacency, and made inquiries of the huntsmen relative to this regiment. They spoke very disparagingly of the superior officers, and very highly of the subalterns. At last Batourine, still through the huntsmen, asked to be presented to the Grand Duke, at the chase. To this the Duke was not altogether favourable at first, but at last he consented. By little and little it was so managed that the Duke, while hunting one day, met Batourine in a retired spot. Batourine on seeing him, fell on his knees, and swore to acknowledge no other master but him, and to do whatever he commanded. The Grand Duke told me that on hearing this oath he became very much alarmed, gave both spurs to his horse, and left Batourine on his knees in the wood. The huntsmen, he said, were in advance, and did not hear what had been said. He pretended that this was all the connection he had had with the man, and that he had even advised the huntsmen to take care that he did not get them into mischief. His present anxiety was occasioned by his learning from the huntsmen that Batourine had been arrested and transferred to Preobrajenskoe, where the Secret Chancery, which took cognizance of crimes against the state, was established. His Imperial Highness trembled for the huntsmen, and was very much afraid of being himself compromised. As far as the former were concerned, his fears were realized; for, a few days afterwards, they were arrested and conducted to Preobrajenskoe. I endeavoured to diminish his distress by representing to him, that if he really had not entered into any parley beyond what he had mentioned, it appeared to me that, at the worst, he had only been guilty of an imprudence, in mixing himself up with such bad company. I cannot say whether he told me the truth. I have reason to believe that he attenuated what there might be of parleying in the affair, for even to me he spoke about the matter in broken sentences, and as if unwillingly. However, the excessive fear he was in might also have produced this same effect upon him. A short time afterwards he came to tell me that some huntsmen had been set at liberty, but with an order to be conveyed beyond the frontier, and that they had sent him word that they had not mentioned his name. This information delighted him beyond measure; his mind became at ease, and no more was heard of the matter. As for Batourine, he was found very culpable. I have not since read or seen the account of his examination, but I have learned that he meditated nothing less than to kill the Empress, to set fire to the palace, and in the horror and confusion to place the Grand Duke on the throne. He was condemned, after being subjected to the torture, to pass the remainder of his days shut up in the fortress of Schlusselburg. Having, during my reign, endeavoured to make his escape from this prison, he was sent to Kamtchatka, whence he fled with Benjousky, and was killed while pillaging *en passant* the island of Formosa, in the Pacific Ocean.

(Continue on the second volume)

РИСУНКИ

Одежды и Вооруженія

РОССІЙСКИХЪ

ВОЙСКЪ.

PLATES LIST OF ILLUSTRATIONS

551. 3 general officer from 1764 to 1786.
552. Field Marshal, from 1764 to 1786.
553. Brigadier saddlecloth of Chushka Cheprakov from 1764 to 1796
554. Saddle cloth of Mallorcan General and General Poruchichi from 1764 to 1796.
555. Saddle cloth of General Anshefskie and General Feldmarshalskie from 1764 to 1796.
556. The General's adjutant and General from 1764 to 1780.
557. Saddle: Adjutant and Adjutant General Field Infantry.
558. Dragoon Regiment, from 1764 to 1775
559. Dragoon: Guns from 1764 to 1796 and Palash from 1764 to 1777
560. Corporal and NCO officers Dragoon Regiment, from 1764 to 1775.
561. Trumpeter Dragoon Regiment, from 1764 to 1775.
562. Kettledrummer Dragoon Regiment, from 1764 to 1775.
563. Sergeants and privates Artillery command at regiment of dragoons, from 1764 to 1775.
564. Chief officer Dragoon Regiment, from 1764 to 1775.
565. Officer Dragoon Regiment, from 1764 to 1775.
566. Colonel Dragoon Regiment, from 1764 to 1775.
567. The shoulder straps or epaulettes Dragoons, from 1764-1775.
568. The shoulder straps or epaulettes Dragoons, from 1764-1775.
569. Emblems of the Dragoons. Dragoon: Sabre from 1775 and 1786.
570. Senior officers and non-commissioned officers Dragoon Regiment, from 1775 on 1786
571. Dragoon saddle cloth from 1775 to 1796.
572. Private, trumpeter and chief officer Dragoon Regiment, from 1786 to 1796.
573. Trumpeter Dragoon regiment in the army of Prince Potemkin, 1788-1791.
574. Officer Dragoon regiment in the army of Prince Potemkin, 1788-1791.
575. Private Carabinier Regiment, from 1763 to 1778.
576. Carabinier: Carbine, from 1763 to 1796 and Palash, from 1763 to 1778
577. Carabinier Tubach Regiment, from 1764 to 1778
578. Senior officers, NCO officers and staff officers Carabinier Regiment, from 1763 to 1778.
579. The shoulder straps or epaulettes Carabinier regiments, 1763-1778.
580. The shoulder straps and epaulettes: Carabinier regiments of 1763-1788
581. The shoulder straps and epaulettes: Cuirassier regiments, 1763-1775.
582. Coat: Tyumen Carabinier Regiment in 1764 and Carabinier: Broadsword and Tashkov, 1778-1786
583. Private Carabinier Regiment, from 1776 to 1786.
584. Chief officer Carabinier Regiment, from 1778 to 1786.
585. NCO Carabinier regiment from 1786 to 1796.
586. Officer Carabinier Regiment, from 1786 to 1796.
587. Trumpeter Carabinier Regiment, from 1786 to 1796.
588. Private Cuirassier Regiment, from 1763 to 1778.
589. Breastplate and Tashkov Kürassier, from 1763 to 1778.
590. Trumpeter, senior officers and colonels Cuirassier Regiment, from 1763 to 1778.
591. Officer's Breastplate, from 1763 to 1778.
592. Saddle cloth of Kirasirsky Cheprakov from 1763 to 1778 (chief officer and Staff Officers).
593. Shoulder straps and epaulettes: Cavalry regiments of 1763-1788
594. Private and senior officers of the Military Order Cuirassier Regiment, in 1775, 1776 and 1777 years.
595. Private Novotroitsk Cuirassier Regiment, from 1776 to 1786
596. Cuirassier regiment from 1778 to 1786: Life-Cuirassier staff officer in vsednevnoy form, the Order's chief officer in dress uniform, Kazan Trumpeter and Cuirassier Life series.
597. Officers and men of the Heir Cuirassier Regiment, from 1778 to 1796.
598. Private Life-Cuirassier Regiment, from 1786 to 1796.
599. Kettledrummer Life Cuirassier Cuirassier trumpeters and Military Order of the regiment from 1786 to 1796
600. Corporal Ekaterinoslav and Private Kazan Cuirassier regiments, from 1786 to 1796.
601. Landmilitskoy Grenadier Corps, from 1763 to the year 1770.
602. Gunners Landmilitskogo Infantry Regiment from 1763 to the year 1770.
603. Officers Landmilitskoy Corps, from 1764 to 1770
604. Emblems: Ukrainian Landmilitskih regiments, 1765
605. Shoulder straps and epaulettes: of 1763-1770.
606. Shoulder straps and epaulettes: of 1763-1770.
607. Shoulder straps and epaulettes: of 1763-1770.
608. Shoulder straps and epaulettes: of 1763-1770.

Private Musketeers Infantry Regiment from 1763 to 1786. (In the form of Infantry).

Musketeers from 1763 to 1786. (In uniform).

Corporal and Musketeer mounted officer Infantry Regiment from 1763 to 1786

497

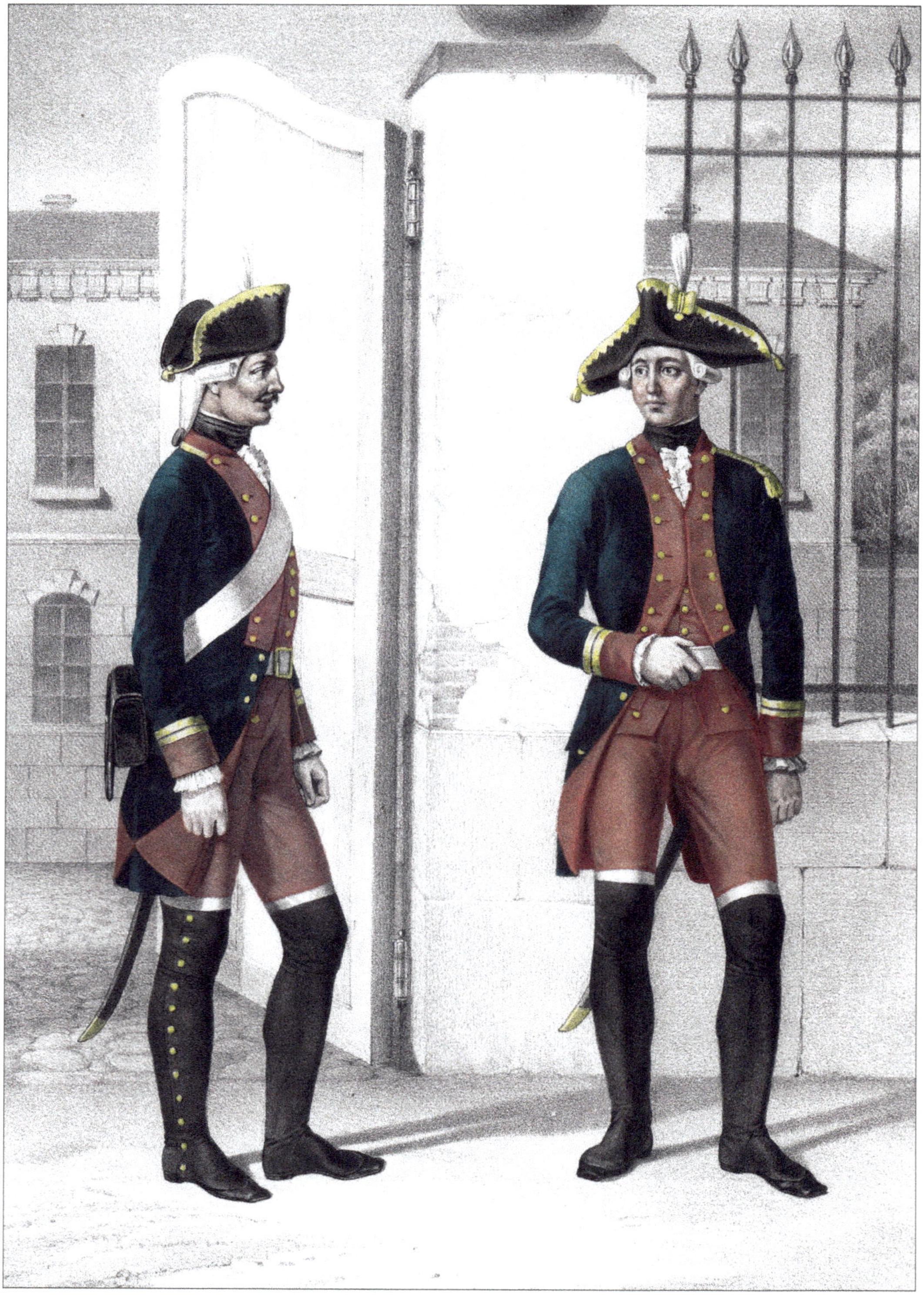

Storekeeper and Ensigns Musketeer officer Infantry Regiment from 1763 to 1786

Corporal sergeant grenadier and private Infantry Regiment from 1763 to 1786.

Grenadier Hat, from 1763 to 1775.

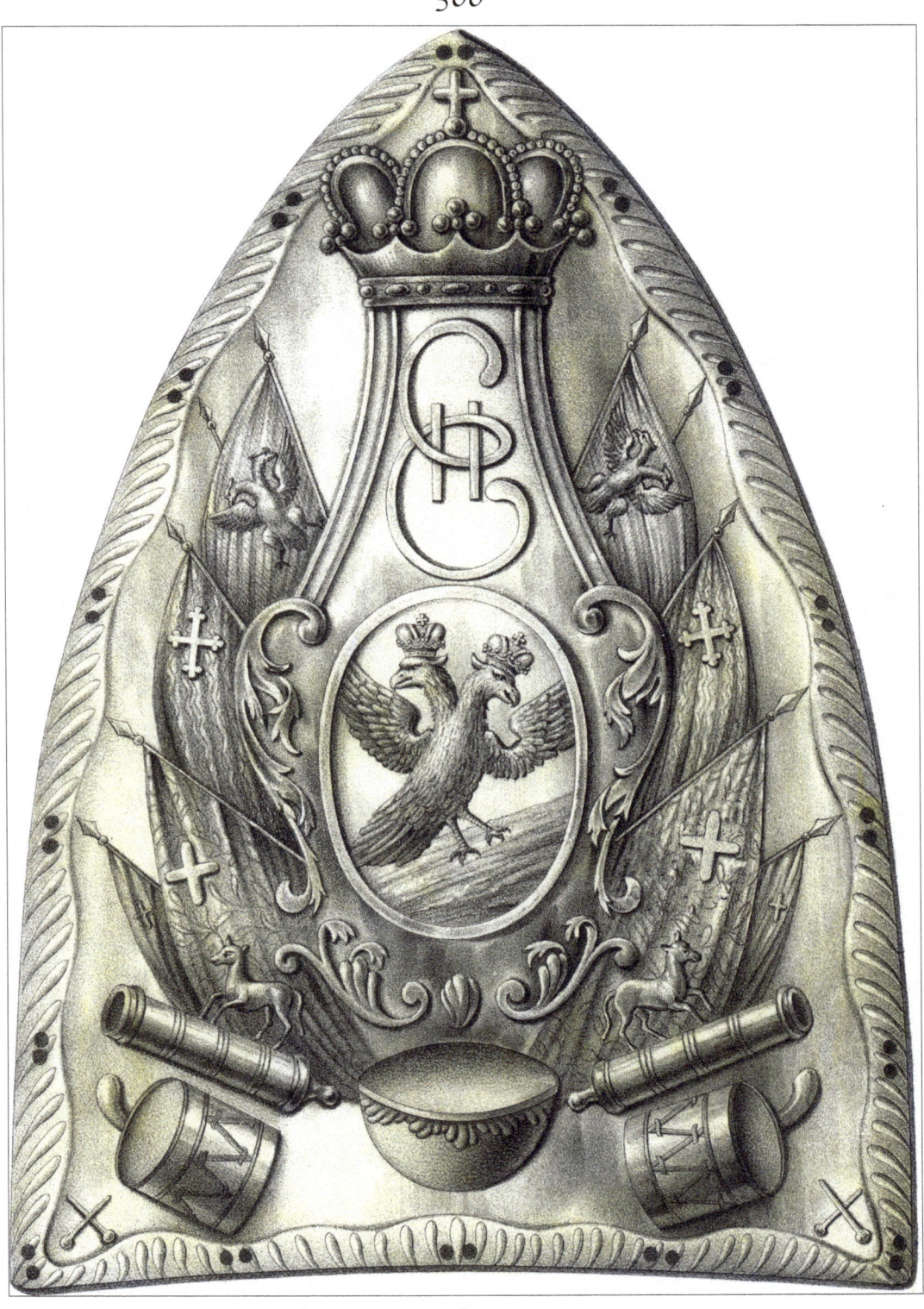

Plaque on grenadier cap, 1763-1775.

Fusilier of an Artillery command at Infantry Regiment, from 1763 to 1786

Artillery Gunners team at Infantry Regiment, from 1763 to 1786

High officer Infantry Regiment from 1763 to 1786. (Marching in parade uniform).

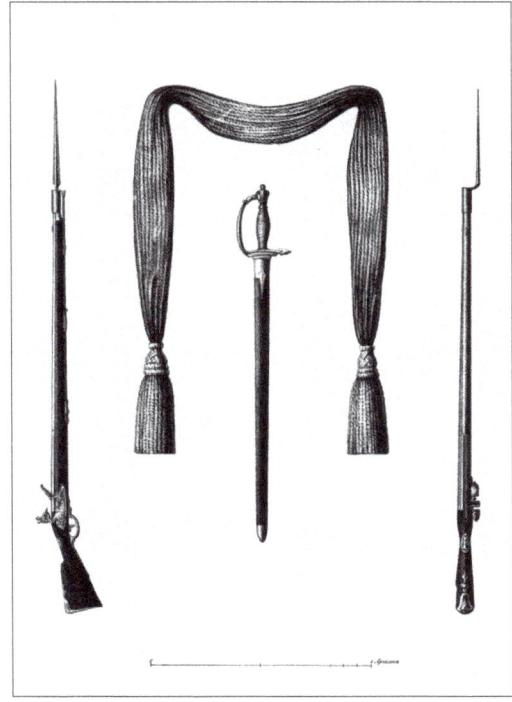
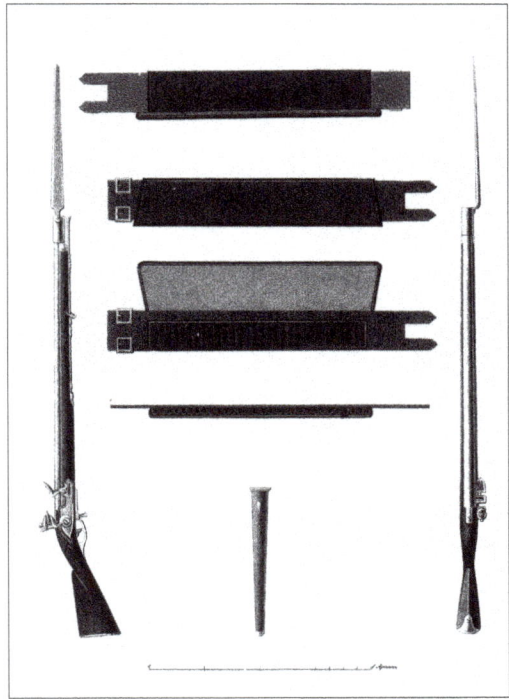
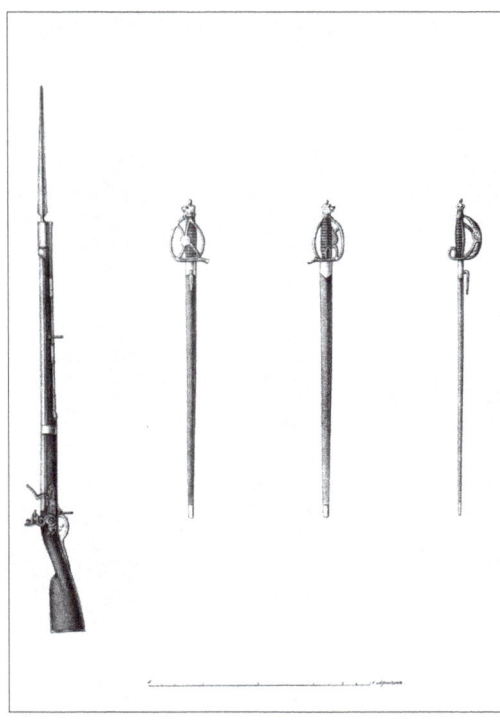
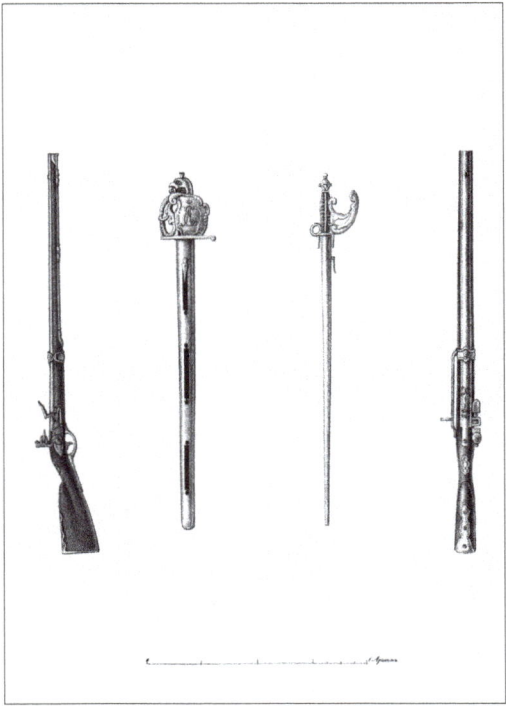

Army infantry officer: rifle or shotgun and scarf from 1763 to 1796 and a sword from 1763 to 1786

High Army infantry officer from 1763-1786

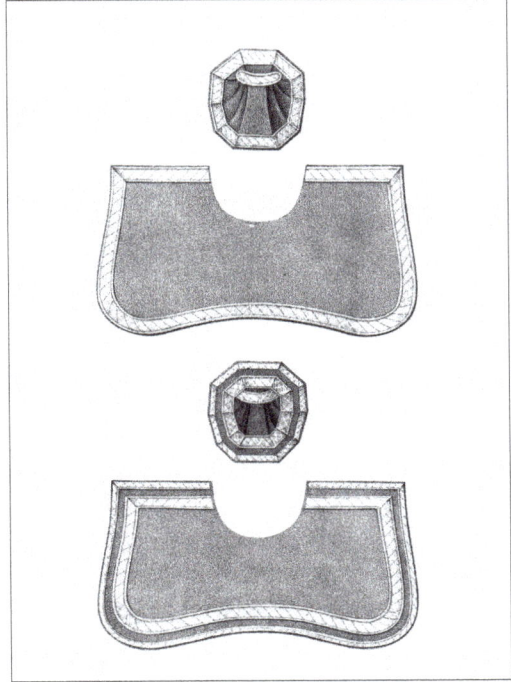

Saddlecloth and horse pockets of Infantry and staff officer from 1764 to 1796. - Brigadier saddlecloth of Chushka Cheprakov from 1764 to 1796 - Saddle cloth of Mallorcan General and General Poruchichi from 1764 to 1796. - Saddle cloth of General Anshefskie and General Feldmarshalskie from 1764 to 1796.

Drummer and Musician Infantry Regiment from 1763 to 1786.

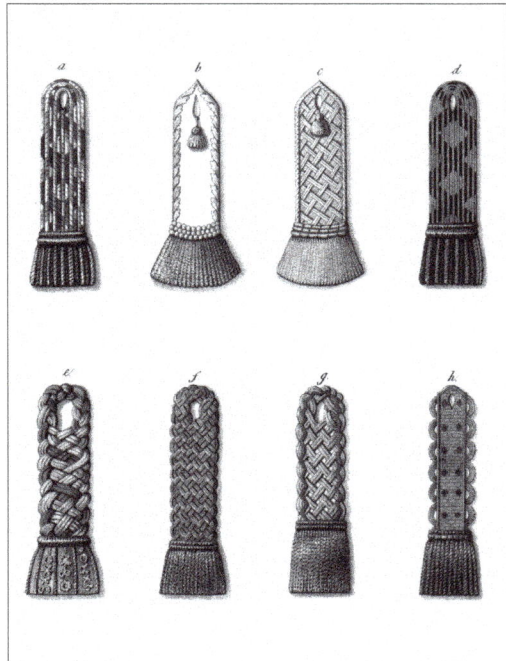
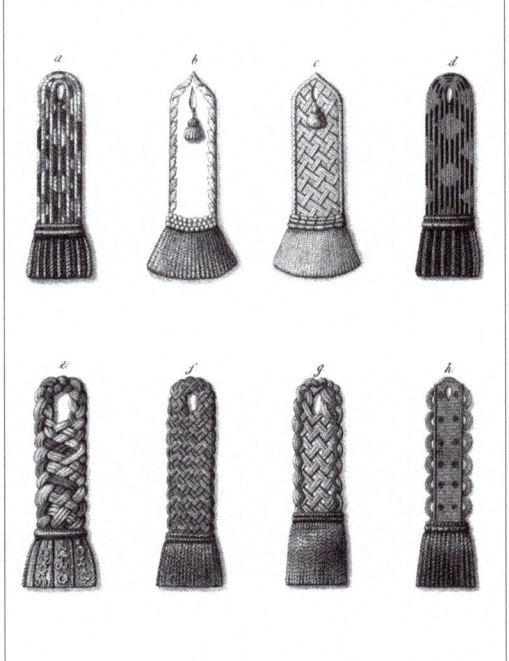

Shoulder straps or epaulettes Infantry Regiment, 1763-1796. -

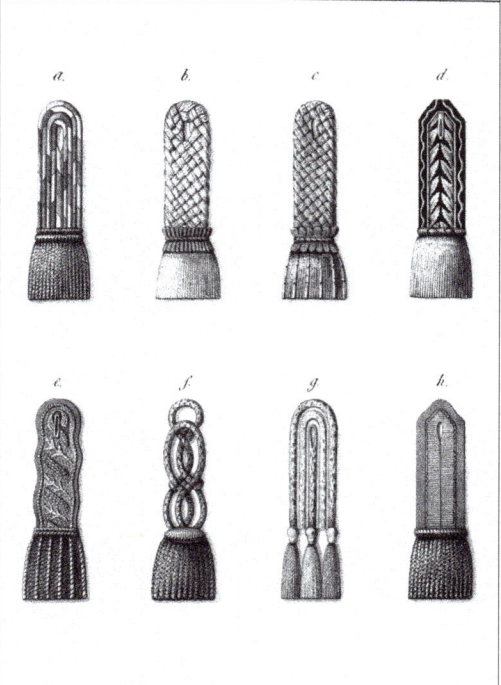

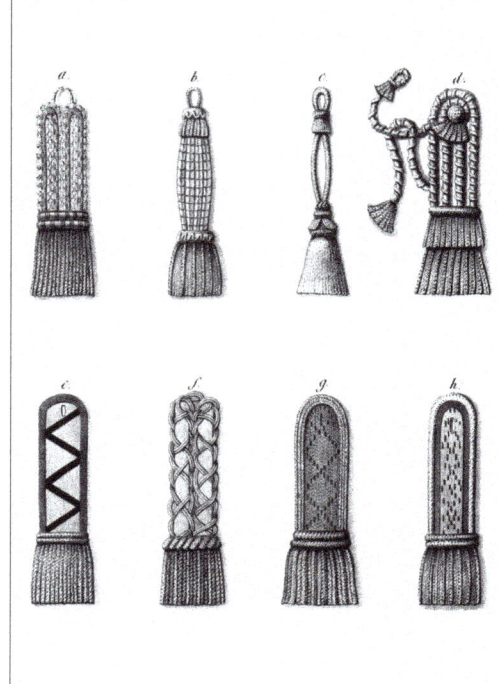

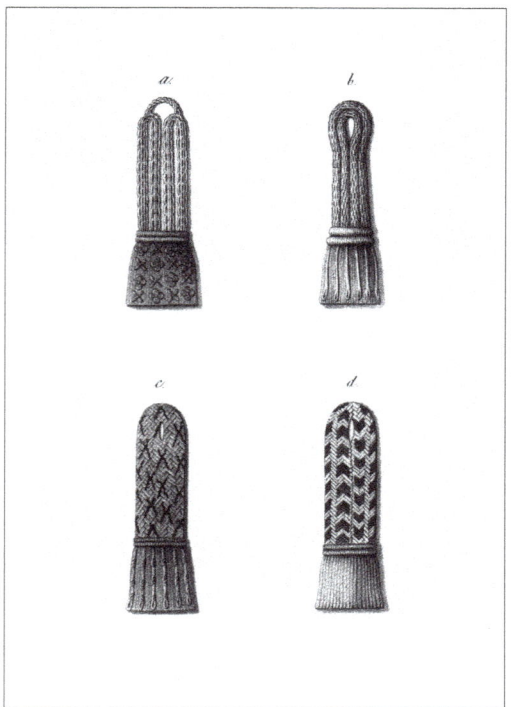

Shoulder straps or epaulettes Infantry Regiment, 1763-1796. - Aguilletes lower ranks, from 1775 to 1796

NCO Infantry Regiment from 1763 to 1786.

Cabby Infantry Regiment from 1763 to 1786.

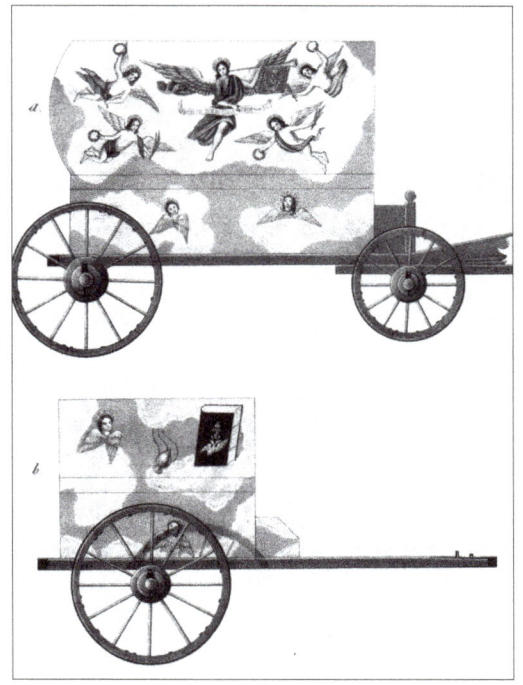

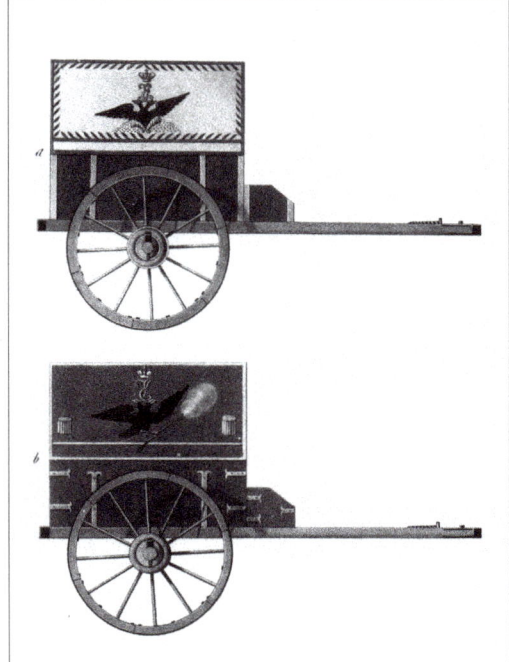

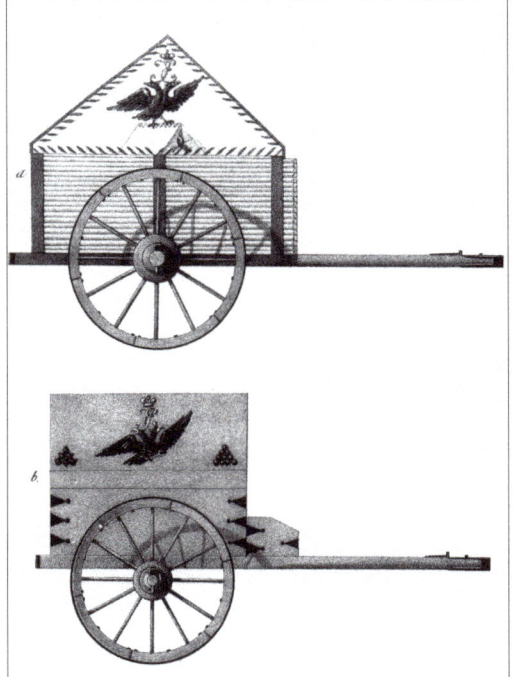

Church drawers Infantry Regiment in 1763. - Magazine drawers Infantry Regiment in 1763. - Ammunitions drawers Infantry Regiment in 1763. - Tent and artillery boxes, 1763.

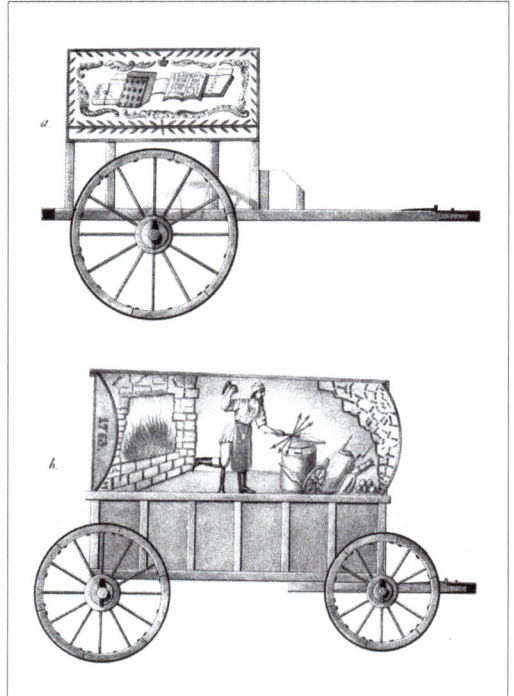

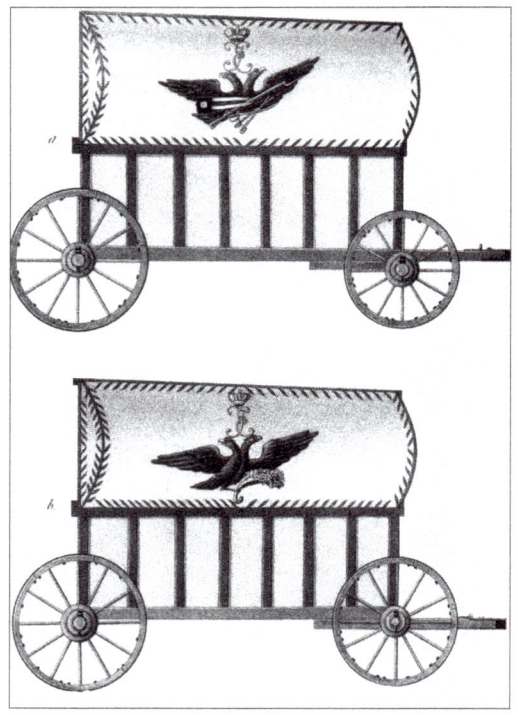

Stationery box and Forge wagon Infantry Regiment, 1763. - Treasury and magazine trucks Infantry Regiment in 1763. - Coats of arms of Dniester, Polotsk and Tula Infantry Regiment, 1776 - Emblems: Irkutsk, Nerchinsk and Selenga Infantry Regiment, 1764

Infantry officer from 1764 to 1796.

Plaque on grenadier caps, with 1775 to 1786.

Private soldier Musketeer Regiment, from 1768 to 1796.

Musketeer helmet from 1786 to 1796.

Musketeer helmet from 1786 to 1796.

Grenadier Musketeer Regiment, from 1786 to 1796

Gunners and Colonel Infantry Regiment from 1786 to 1796.

Drummer and Musician Infantry Regiment from 1786 to 1796

Cabby Infantry Regiment from 1786 to 1796.

Noncombatants and cabbies Infantry Regiment from 1786 to 1796.

Officers Infantry Regiment in the army of Prince Potemkin 1788-1791.

Infantry officer's badge, 1788-1796.

Privates and non-commissioned officers of the Grenadier Regiment, from 1786 to 1796.

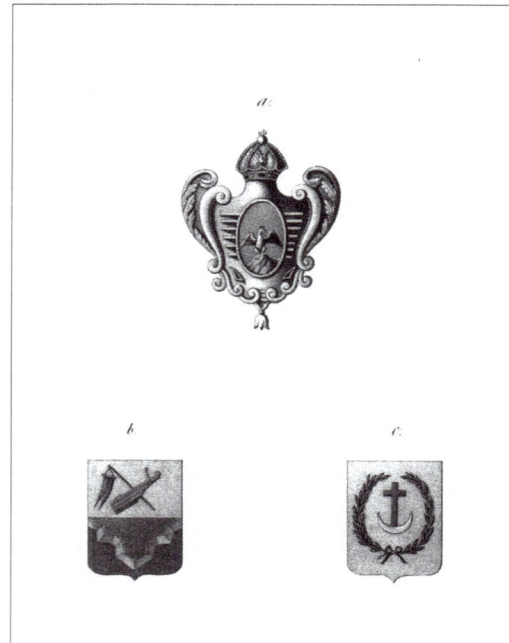

Emblems of the field battalions, 1776. - Generals sewing, from 1764 to 1796. - Emblems of the Dragoons. Dragoon: Sabre from 1775 and 1786. - Emblems: Ukrainian Landmilitskih regiments, 1765

Rows of Jaeger, from 1765 to 1786

Jaeger non-commissioned officer from 1765 to 1777

Jaeger drummer from 1765 to 1777

Senior officers and sergeants Chasseur Battalion, from 1777 to 1786.

546

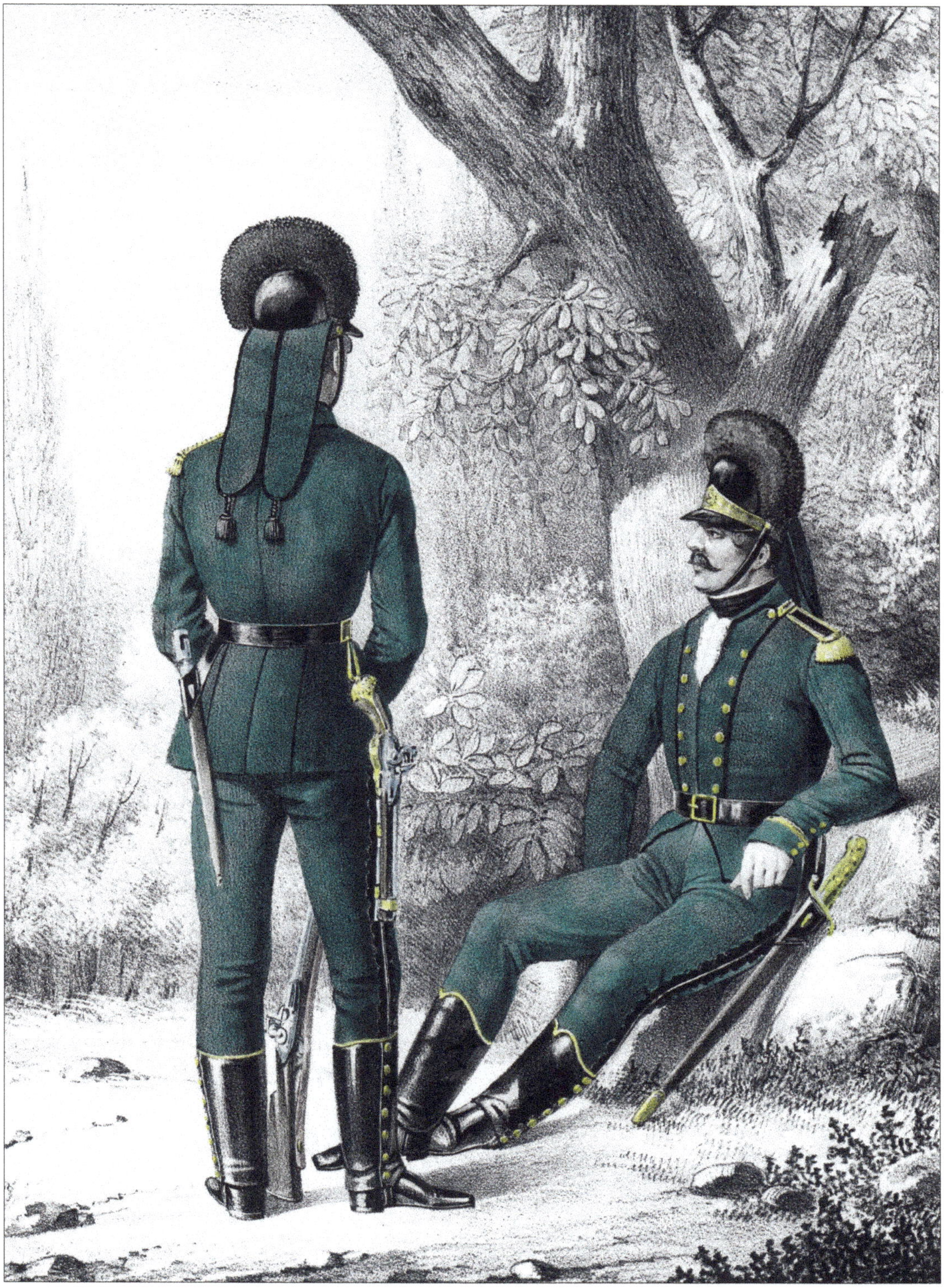

Jaeger: enlisted men from 1786 to 1796.

Jaeger trumpeter from 1786 to 1796.

548

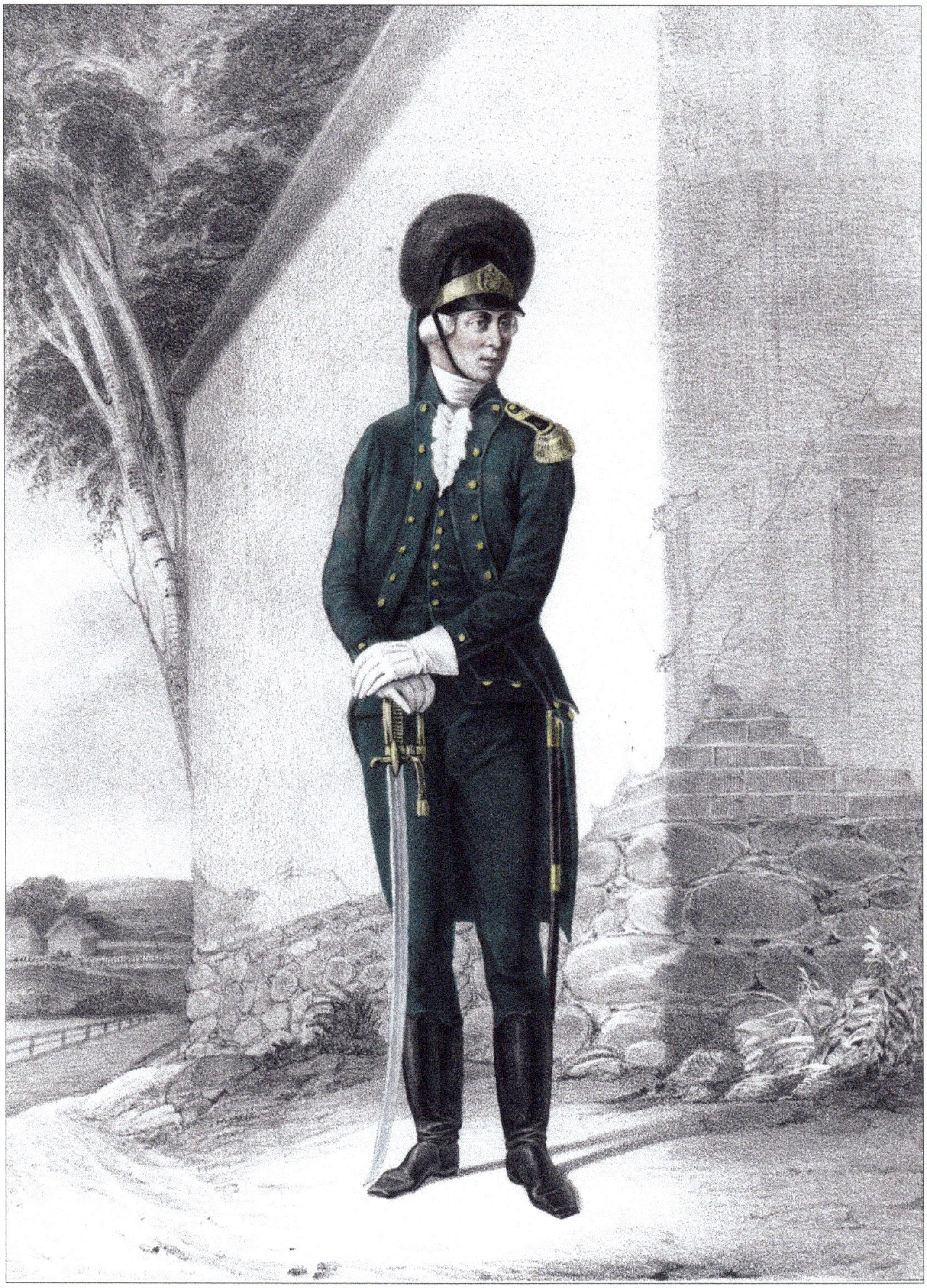

Jaeger officer from 1786 to 1796.

Brigadier from 1764 to 1786.

3 general officer from 1764 to 1786.

Field Marshal, from 1764 to 1786.

The General's adjutant and General from 1764 to 1780.

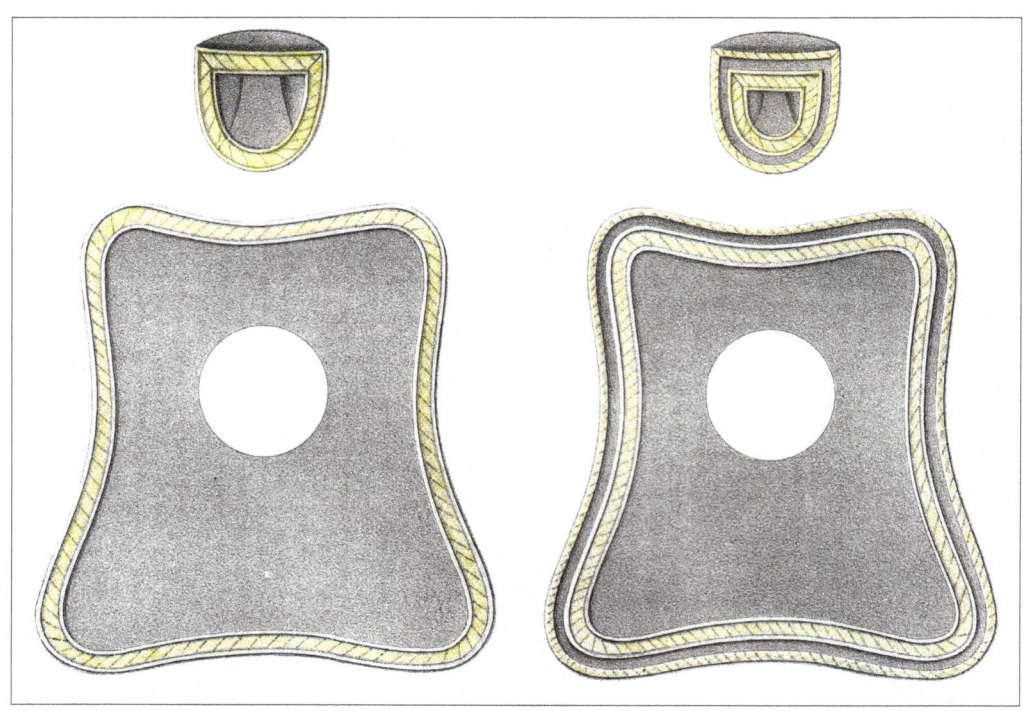

Saddle: Adjutant and Adjutant General Field Infantry. - Officer's Breastplate, from 1763 to 1778.

Dragoon Regiment, from 1764 to 1775

Corporal and NCO officers Dragoon Regiment, from 1764 to 1775.

Trumpeter Dragoon Regiment, from 1764 to 1775.

Kettledrummer Dragoon Regiment, from 1764 to 1775.

Sergeants and privates Artillery command at regiment of dragoons, from 1764 to 1775.

Chief officer Dragoon Regiment, from 1764 to 1775.

Officer Dragoon Regiment, from 1764 to 1775.

Colonel Dragoon Regiment, from 1764 to 1775.

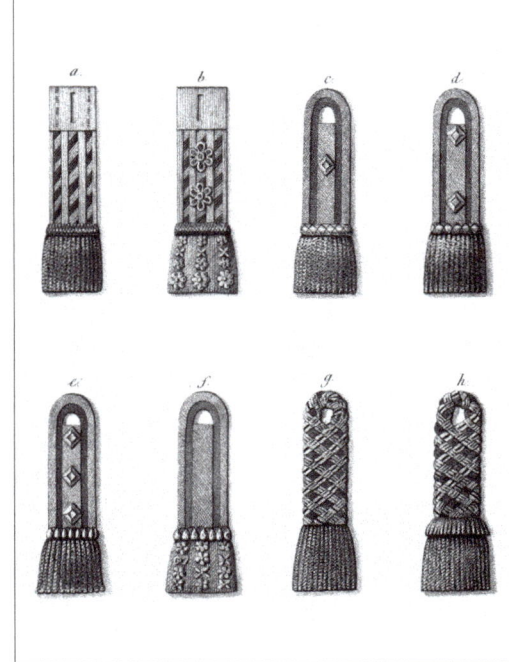
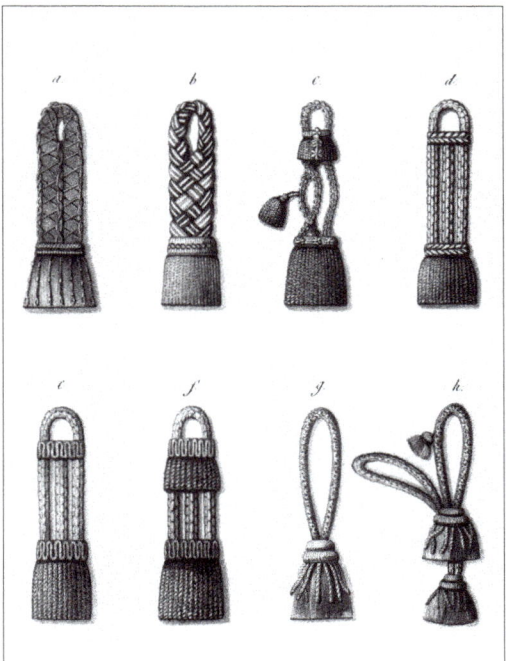
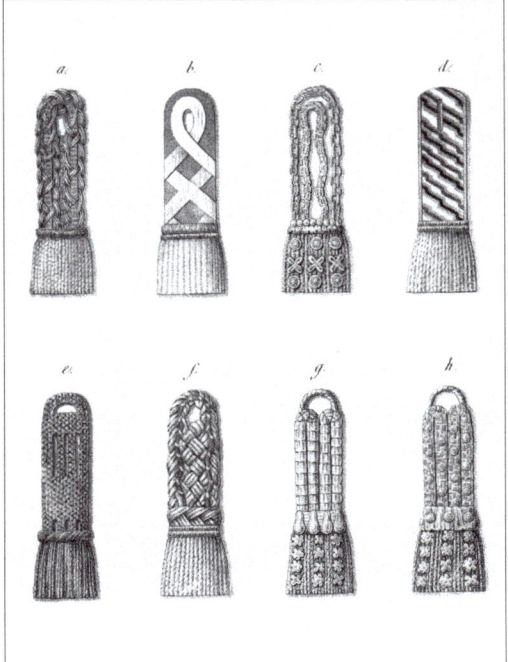

The shoulder straps or epaulettes Dragoons, from 1764-1775. 1 & 2 - The shoulder straps and epaulettes: Carabinier regiments of 1763-1788 1 & 2.

Senior officers and non-commissioned officers Dragoon Regiment, from 1775 on 1786

a.

b.

Dragoon saddle cloth from 1775 to 1796.

Private, trumpeter and chief officer Dragoon Regiment, from 1786 to 1796.

Trumpeter Dragoon regiment in the army of Prince Potemkin, 1788-1791.

574

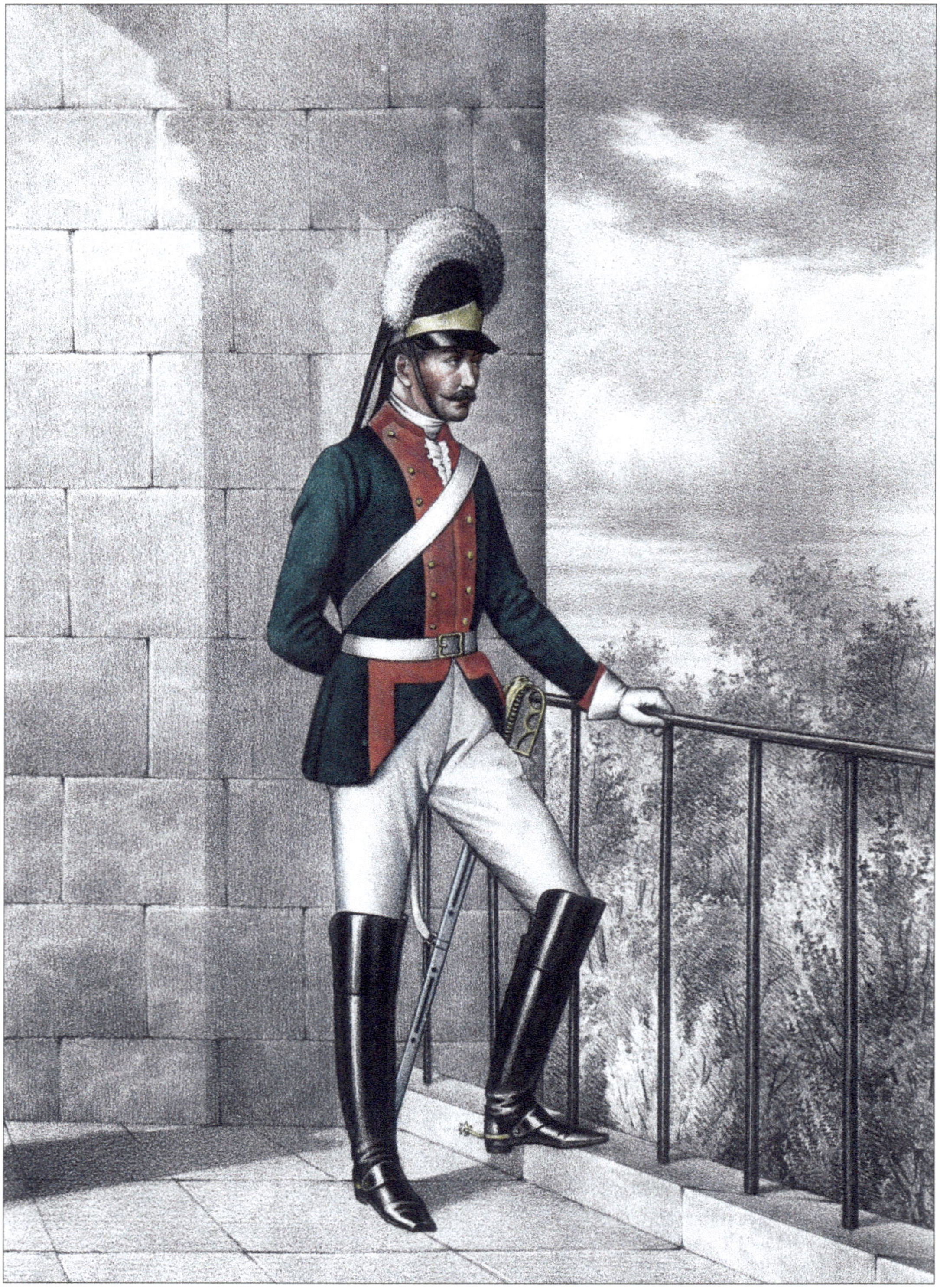

Officer Dragoon regiment in the army of Prince Potemkin, 1788-1791.

Private Carabinier Regiment, from 1763 to 1778.

Carabinier Tubach Regiment, from 1764 to 1778

Senior officers, NCO officers and staff officers Carabinier Regiment, from 1763 to 1778.

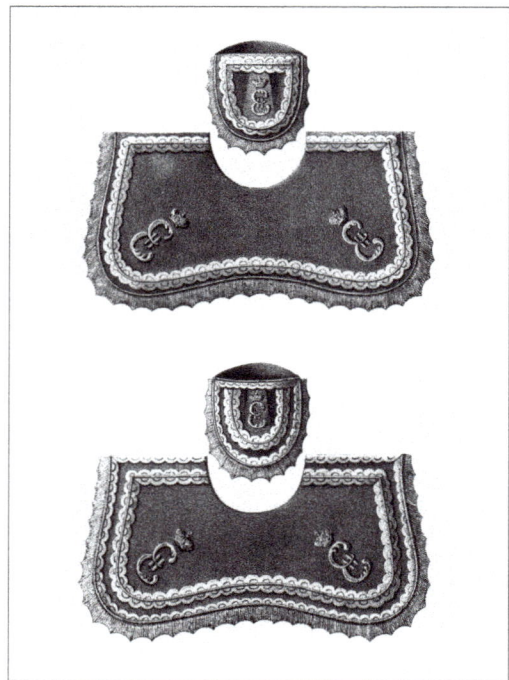

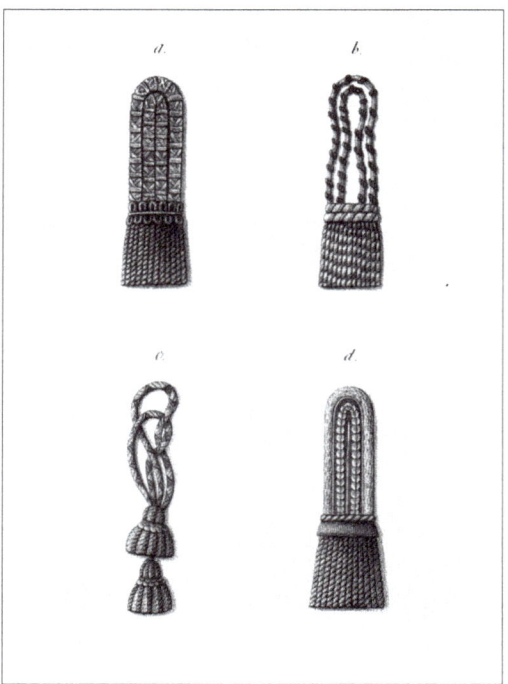

The shoulder straps and epaulettes: Cuirassier regiments, 1763-1775. - Coat: Tyumen Carabinier Regiment in 1764 and Carabinier: Broadsword and Tashkov, 1778-1786 - Saddle cloth of Kirasirsky Cheprakov from 1763 to 1778 (chief officer and Staff Officers). - Shoulder straps and epaulettes: Cavalry regiments of 1763-1788

Private Carabinier Regiment, from 1776 to 1786.

Chief officer Carabinier Regiment, from 1778 to 1786.

NCO Carabinier regiment from 1786 to 1796.

Trumpeter Carabinier Regiment, from 1786 to 1796.

Trumpeter Carabinier Regiment, from 1786 to 1796.

Private Cuirassier Regiment, from 1763 to 1778.

Breastplate and Tashkov Kürassier, from 1763 to 1778.

Trumpeter, senior officers and colonels Cuirassier Regiment, from 1763 to 1778.

Private and senior officers of the Military Order Cuirassier Regiment, in 1775, 1776 and 1777 years.

Private Novotroitsk Cuirassier Regiment, from 1776 to 1786

Cuirassier regiment from 1778 to 1786: Life-Cuirassier staff officer in vsednevnoy form, the Order's chief officer in dress uniform, Kazan Trumpeter and Cuirassier Life series.

Officers and men of the Heir Cuirassier Regiment, from 1778 to 1796.

Private Life-Cuirassier Regiment, from 1786 to 1796.

Kettledrummer Life Cuirassier & trumpeters and Military Order of the regiment from 1786 to 1796

Corporal Ekaterinoslav and Private Kazan Cuirassier regiments, from 1786 to 1796.

Landmilitskoy Grenadier Corps, from 1763 to the year 1770.

Gunners Landmilitskogo Infantry Regiment from 1763 to the year 1770.

Officers Landmilitskoy Corps, from 1764 to 1770

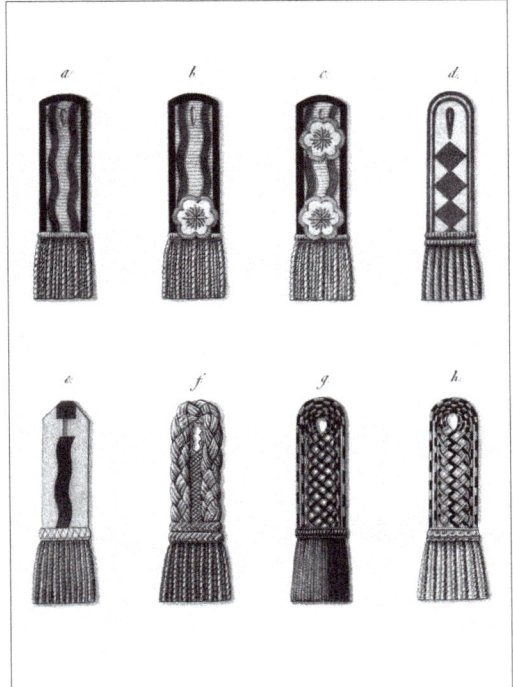

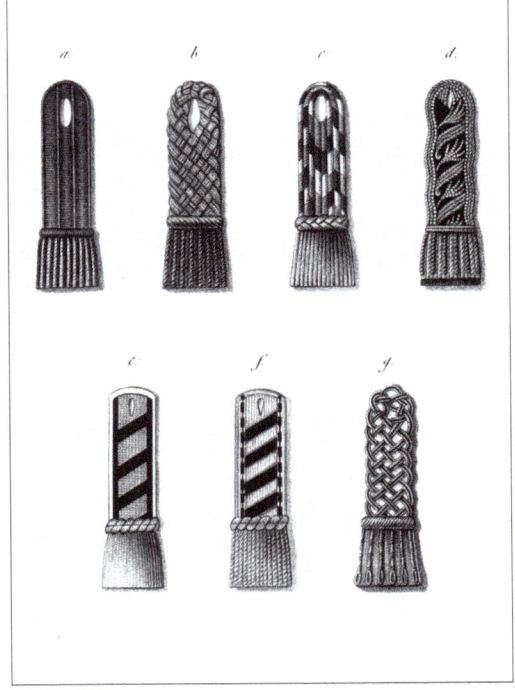

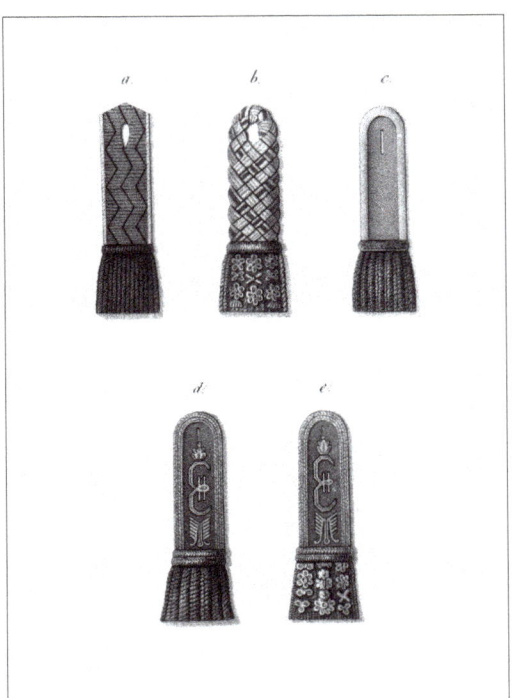

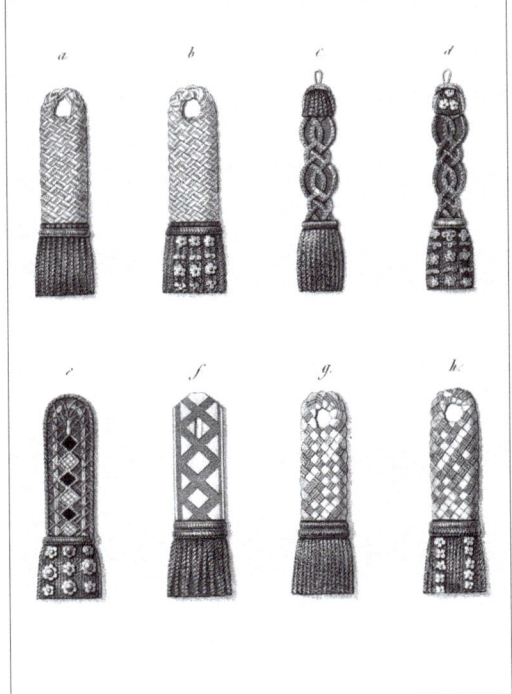

Shoulder straps and epaulettes: of 1763-1770.

SOLDIERS, WEAPONS & UNIFORMS ALREADY PUBLISHED
(SOME TITLES)

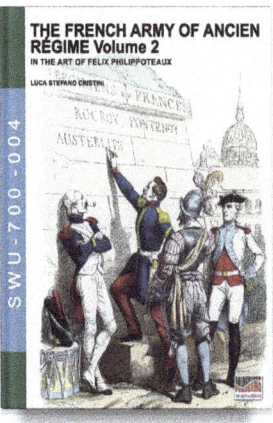
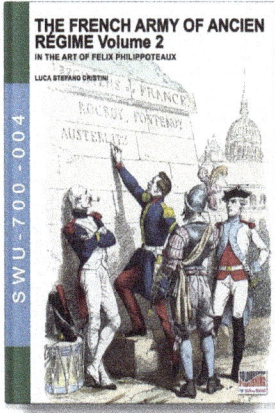
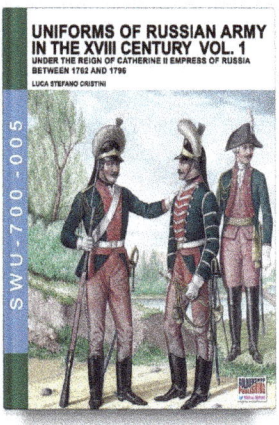

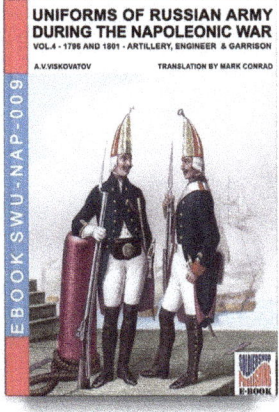

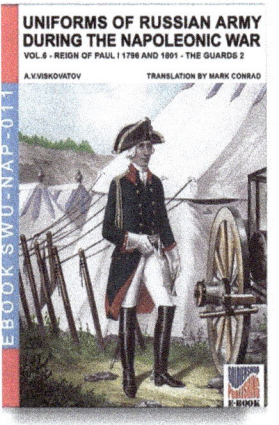

www.ingramcontent.com/pod-product-compliance
Lightning Source LLC
Chambersburg PA
CBHW041143120626
46547CB00020B/3093